My Christmas Stocking

This edition published in 1993 by SMITHMARK Publishers Inc.
16 East 32nd Street, New York, NY 10016

ISBN 0-8317-5173-8

MY CHRISTMAS STOCKING
Stories, Songs, Poems, Recipes, Crafts, and Fun for Kids
was prepared and produced by
Magnolia Editions Limited
15 West 26th Street
New York, NY 10010

Editor: Karla Olson
Art Director: Jeff Batzli
Photography Editor: Anne K. Price
Production Manager: Jeanne E. Kaufman
Line Illustrations by Charles Donahue

Typeset by Bookworks Plus
Color separations by Bright Arts (Hong Kong) Pte. Ltd.
Printed in Hong Kong and bound in China by Leefung-Asco Printers Ltd.

SMITHMARK Books are available for bulk purchase for sales promotion and premium
use. For details write or call the manager of special sales, SMITHMARK Publishers Inc.,
16 East 32nd Street, New York, NY 10016; (212) 532-6600.

My Christmas Stocking

Stories, Songs, Poems, Recipes, Crafts, and Fun for Kids

Dan Elish
Illustrations by James Bernardin
Photographs by Nancy Palubulak
Crafts by Alexandra Eames

SMITHMARK

C o n t e n t s

Introduction

CHRISTMAS IS ONE OF THE WORLD'S MOST LOVED HOLIDAYS, A DAY TO SING carols, exchange presents, and celebrate with your family. It is a day you anticipate for many weeks, beginning with choosing your Christmas tree and ending with your favorite dessert from a grand Christmas dinner. This book is meant to help you celebrate this special holiday and to be your companion year in and year out.

My Christmas Stocking is a terrific collection of stories, lore, recipes, and crafts to bring you Christmas cheer. Find out who the "real" Santa was; how to make a plate of Christmas cookies; how the tradition of the Christmas tree began. It's all here, waiting for you. So now that the air is cool and crisp with the smell of the Christmas season, turn the pages full of fun for the greatest day of the year.

CHAPTER ONE

Evergreens

"Today we'll pick out our Christmas tree!"
When you hear those words, you know Christmas is coming!

You and your family bundle up, head out to the corner Christmas tree lot or farm, and the annual Christmas tree argument begins. Each member of the family has a different idea of the perfect tree. Your sister wants a tall one, while your brother favors one with sturdier branches. But while they're arguing, you notice the best one of all—tall, green, and full. After inspecting it from every angle, the choice is finally made. You cart the tree home—*your* tree, one that seems to be especially right for your family.

The first thing you notice is the crisp smell of fresh pine when the tree is carried into the house. Then, the magic of decorating begins. You pull the strings of lights out of the closet, spread them across the living room (and sometimes down the hall), and untangle them. (Of course, some lights have burned out and need to be replaced.) You thread popcorn and cranberries onto string, creating different patterns by alternating them. You blow dust off the boxes of ornaments, then open them to reveal their treasures. Many of these ornaments have been in your family for generations, and they are as familiar as old friends. For many of you, one of the most exciting parts of Christmas is choosing (or even making) a new ornament each year; here are all your ornaments from years past, ready to adorn your beautiful new tree.

After the tree is fully decorated and draped with shining tinsel, you turn on the blue, red, and green lights—it's a magical moment. Your eyes light up with wonder, and the living room takes on a warm Christmastime glow.

Wandering through snowy woods
To find the perfect evergreen
In the distance, there it stood,
The greenest one I'd ever seen.
I raised my arms, gave a mighty whack
Then lugged it home upon my back,
To show my waiting family
Our evergreen—our Christmas tree.

—Anonymous

O Christmas Tree

O Christmas tree, O Christmas tree,
How lovely are your branches.
In summer sun, in winter snow,
A dress of green you always show.
O Christmas tree, O Christmas tree,
How lovely are your branches.

O Christmas tree, O Christmas tree,
With happiness we greet you.
When decked with candles once a year,
You fill our hearts with yuletide cheer.
O Christmas tree, O Christmas tree,
With happiness we greet you.

Having stuffed our burlap sacks with enough greenery and crimson to garland a dozen windows, we set about choosing a tree. "It should be," muses my friend, "twice as tall as a boy. So a boy can't steal the star."

—Truman Capote,
A Christmas Memory

During the days before and after Christmas, neighbors drop by, some bringing more ornaments.

By Christmas Eve, the tree is a thing of beauty—sparkling and ready for the gifts from brothers, sisters, parents, uncles, aunts, neighbors, and, last but not least, Santa.

Many legends of the tree have been passed down through the years. One is that the lights on the tree are the stars in the sky and the star on top is the one that led the three wise men to the baby Jesus.

Another tale is of a poor woodman and his wife who took pity on a shivering boy one Christmas Eve and gave him a full meal and a warm bed. In the morning, beautiful music filled the house and their tree was covered with shining lights and glittering ornaments. The poor boy was the Christ Child, who returned the couple's kindness with a bright tree that warmed their home each year at Christmas.

Another legend tells of a good woman who spent hours trimming her tree. During the night, spiders crawled from branch to branch, leaving behind their beautiful webs. The Christ Child blessed the tree to reward the woman for her goodness and, in the morning, the webs were transformed into pure, brightly shining silver—tinsel!

Every year, each family knows their tree is the best and the most beautiful. The decorated tree, shining with tinsel, gleaming with flickering lights, sparkling with ornaments, is one of the most enchanting traditions of the holiday.

The people of Germany and Scandinavia were the first to bring trees into their homes. They brought in evergreens to put a little springtime into their wood cabins during the cold winter months. Eventually, they decorated the trees with paper cutouts and fruit, and perched a candle on top.

Where do Christmas trees come from? Are they chopped down in the forest? No. Today, most trees are carefully raised on farms, then shipped out all over the country. It takes about eight years to grow an average-size tree.

Cookie Cutter Ornaments

Use your Christmas cookie cutters to trace the shapes for Christmas tree ornaments made of felt, then decorate them with sequins, beads, and glitter. If you do not have cookie cutters, draw your own shapes right on the felt and decorate them the same way. You might want to tie an ornament to a gift as a decoration.

MATERIALS:

Felt

Cookie cutters

Felt-tip pen

Scissors

Gold cord

Craft glue

Sequins, spangles, and beads

Glitter

1. Fold felt in half to make a double layer. Lay a cookie cutter on the felt and trace around it with a felt-tip pen. Cut out the shape, cutting through both layers of felt.

2. Make a loop of gold cord and put some glue on the ends of the strand. Open the felt shapes like a sandwich, spread glue on one side, lay the tip of the gold loop near the top, then lay the two pieces together again.

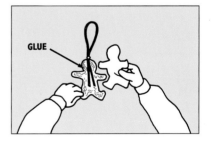

3. Decorate the felt shapes by gluing on sequins and beads. Sprinkle glitter in the glue for extra sparkle.

The Turquoise Ornament

"It's true!" Molly said.

Her older brother shook his head. "Boy, you're dumb!"

"Listen, Ray," Molly went on. "Uncle Mo told me that when a kid has been extra-specially good, Santa always leaves a bright glittery ornament on the tree. It's true!"

"You're even thicker than I thought," Ray said. "First of all, every fifth grader knows that Santa Claus does not exist. That he's merely a legend—a made-up fat guy who takes his red outfit out of the closet once a year and prances around the world on a sleigh. Second, even if such an imaginary person did exist, he would only deliver gifts, not ornaments, because it is a well-known fact that Santa leaves Christmas tree decorations to individual families."

Molly sighed and looked at their family tree. It was beautiful, covered with tinsel, lace, strings of popcorn, little plastic soldiers, and ornaments of all shapes and sizes, twirling and jiggling. Stockings hung over the fireplace, one with her name stitched on in bright green lettering. Everything was set for Christmas Eve.

"And third of all!" Ray continued. . . .

Molly looked back to her brother. "You mean there's more?"

"Yes," Ray went on. "Even if Santa did bring some sort of special ornament to give to a special person, he would most definitely not pick you, because I, as your brother, happen to know as a certified fact, that you are most definitely not extra-specially good in any way. In fact, you are a little brat!"

"I am not!"

But Ray was already out of the room, leaving Molly alone with the beautiful Christmas tree. She had been good. She knew it. Didn't she make her bed every day? Didn't she do the dishes? And once, last July, she had even helped her mother clean out the fish tank.

She was going to get an ornament. Uncle Mo wouldn't lie.

Later, Ray was in the living room, admiring the tree. His great-uncle Mo, a large man with bright green eyes, came around the corner and bent a long finger toward him.

"Hey, you!"

"What?" Ray asked.

Mo winked. "Don't be so hard on your sister, Ray."

"Aw. . ."

Mo raised a hand. His eyes sparkled. "I'm not gonna give you a lecture, boy. Come here . . . closer . . . that's right." The old man leaned forward and whispered in Ray's ear. "You know, when you were in first grade you thought Santa was just as real as your sister does!"

"I did?"

"Yes sir! Now, listen carefully. I made up that little story about the ornament for Molly. What do you say we give little Molly a surprise, eh? A Christmas she'll never forget?"

Ray leaned forward. "What do you have in mind?"

Later that evening, when everyone was asleep, Ray crept to Molly's room and shook her awake.

"What?"

"Get up," Ray whispered. "Don't you hear the reindeer on the roof?"

"Aw, stop being—"

"No! Listen!"

Molly held her breath and listened hard. She wasn't sure, but maybe . . .

"The pitter-patter of hooves!" Ray said. "I think you were right, after all! Come on downstairs!"

Molly stepped into her slippers, crept past her parents' room, followed her brother downstairs, and peered around the corner into the living room. She gasped! It was true! There was Santa! And look! He was placing a bright, turquoise ornament on the tree. It sparkled in the moonlight, glowing in the dim darkness.

Molly took a step forward.

"No," Ray whispered, blocking her with his hand. "Don't let him know you've seen him." He looked at his sister. "You know, I guess you were right. . . ."

Molly's heart pounded. She raced upstairs! It was true! Santa had given her her very own ornament!

Ray watched her go, then turned toward the living room. His uncle took a step forward.

"Did she go for it?" the old man asked.

Ray nodded. "Like a charm." He grinned. "I almost believed you were Santa myself!"

They laughed. "Boy, was she ever excited!"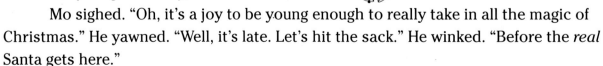

Mo sighed. "Oh, it's a joy to be young enough to really take in all the magic of Christmas." He yawned. "Well, it's late. Let's hit the sack." He winked. "Before the *real* Santa gets here."

"Yeah, *right*." Ray grinned. "You mean before Mom and Dad get up early and put the gifts under the tree."

But then, as the boy and man headed upstairs to bed, Mo stopped suddenly.

"Did you hear something rustling on the roof?" he asked.

Ray scowled. "No way, Mo. That's the same line I used on Molly."

Mo grinned. "You're right. I must be hearing things. Let's get to bed."

The next morning, Ray and Mo woke with the rest of the family. Walking into the living room, Ray's heart jumped.

"Mo?" he said, nodding toward the tree. "Do you see what . . ."

Indeed, Uncle Mo saw what Ray saw. He shook his head in disbelief. Next to the turquoise ornament they had placed on the tree to fool Molly hung another ornament, larger, more beautiful, round and gleaming.

"What lovely ornaments," Molly's mother said. "Did you get them, Uncle Mo?"

Uncle Mo shook his head and smiled. "Nope. It must have been Santa."

"He brought me two?" Molly whispered to her brother.

Ray shrugged. "I guess you've been extra-specially good, after all. And maybe I'll have to be a little better next year."

Ornaments Good Enough to Eat

How would you like to make Christmas tree ornaments good enough to eat? Well, here's your chance.

WHAT YOU'LL NEED:

Your imagination, a toothpick, a knife, a small bow, and some ribbon or string

INGREDIENTS:

1 package of marzipan

1 set of food coloring

3 tablespoons butter

2 cups confectioners' sugar

1/4 teaspoon salt

2 teaspoons vanilla

DIRECTIONS:

1. Take the marzipan out of the package and lay it on the kitchen counter or on a cutting board.

2. Mold the marzipan into whatever shape you want: an elf, a reindeer, a Christmas tree . . . use your imagination. Three different-sized balls, for example, one on top of the other, can make a great snowman. Santa himself can be made with a fat ball for the body, a smaller ball for the head, and four thinner pieces for arms and legs.

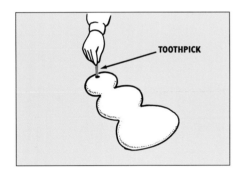

3. Take a toothpick and poke a small hole just large enough to fit a piece of string or ribbon through your ornament (so you can hang it on the tree later on).

4. Let the marzipan harden. This should take just about an hour.

5. While the marzipan is hardening, make the icing: Let the butter soften in a small bowl. Add the confectioners' sugar to the butter, then blend the mixture until it becomes creamy. Add the salt and the vanilla. If your icing is too thin, add more confectioners' sugar; if it's too thick, add a little cream.

6. Separate the icing into several batches, one for each color you want. Blend a few drops of food coloring into each batch, then add a drop or so more until the color is as you like it.

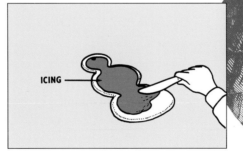

7. Use a toothpick or a knife to smear the icing onto the marzipan. Let the icing dry for 1 hour.

8. When your ornament is fully decorated, wet the end of a piece of string and poke it through the hole.

In Sweden, children often make a straw billy goat to guard the tree. They believe evil spirits may come during the night and take away their decorations.

CHAPTER TWO

Who is Santa Claus?

It's Christmas Eve in the North Pole. In the warmth of his log cabin, Santa Claus fastens the last button on his famous red suit.

Mrs. Claus bustles into the room with a warm glass of apple cider and a plate of sugar cookies.

"Merry Christmas, dear!"

Santa smiles, his green eyes sparkling. "Is everything all set?" he says, his voice round and full.

"The last presents are being lifted onto the sleigh right now!"

Santa takes a quick glance in the mirror, brushes out his thick, white beard, then spins around twice on his heel. "Dear wife," he says, his face alive with excitement. "It's time to deliver some toys!"

Santa and Mrs. Claus open a wood door that leads to the wide-open courtyard, which is crowded with hundreds of elves who have been busy all year in Santa's workshops, making hundreds of handmade gifts. These gifts are now piled high in Santa's sleigh. Pawing the ground before the sleigh, anxious to get to work, are eight reindeer.

Santa waves to the cheering crowd and, with a boost from two elves, climbs onto the sleigh and takes hold of the reins.

"Thank you again!" he cries to the elves. "I couldn't have done it without you!"

There is loud applause, a hush, and then Santa cries, "Yaa!"

The reindeer gallop forward, faster and faster still. When

Old Santeclaus with much delight,
His reindeer drives this frosty night—
O'er chimney-tops and tracks of snow
To bring his yearly gifts to you.

—Anonymous

In 1897, a little girl named Virginia asked her father whether or not Santa Claus really exists. He told her to write to the local newspaper, the <u>New York Sun</u>. This is what she wrote:

Dear Editor:
I am eight years old. Some of my little friends say there is no Santa Claus. Papa says, "If you see it in the <u>Sun</u> it's so." Please tell me the truth, is there a Santa Claus?

Here is the answer from the <u>Sun</u>:

Yes, Virginia, there is a Santa Claus. He exists as certainly as love and generosity and devotion exist, and you know that they abound and give to your life its highest beauty and joy! Alas! How dreary would be the world if there were no Santa Claus. It would be as dreary as if there were no Virginias . . . he will continue to make glad the heart of childhood.

Did you know that each year the post office gets thousands of letters addressed to Santa Claus? Many towns set up special committees that do their best to help Santa answer them all.

Want to visit Santa Claus? Well, you can, though not the person, the <u>place</u>—Santa Claus, Indiana. A small town in Indiana is named after your favorite gift giver. Smack in the middle of the village square is a forty-two-ton, twenty-three-foot-high statue of Saint Nick himself!

Santa lifts the reins, they jump and effortlessly lift the sleigh into the cool, clear night.

Santa's yearly journey has begun.

Every child knows that waiting for Santa to come on Christmas Eve is one of the most exciting parts of the holiday. But who *is* Santa, and how did he get such an important job?

One legend says that over a thousand years ago, a man named Saint Nicholas came to be known throughout the world for his good work and charity. Many people believe that this man is the real Santa Claus. Children in old England called Santa "Father Christmas," and thought he was a gigantic man who wore a scarlet robe and a crown of holly and ivy. German children of yesterday believed that the Christ Child, the *Christkindl* (pronounced KREST-kin-dul), brought their presents on Christmas Eve.

Nowadays, Santa rides his sleigh to the roof and slides down the chimney to put *your* presents under the tree. If you don't have a chimney, don't worry; he or one of his elves will find a way to get inside.

You may want to leave Santa a plate of cookies and a glass of milk to give him the energy he needs for his long night's work. And be sure to ask your parents to put out the fire in the fireplace so he doesn't burn his feet.

As you open your gifts on Christmas morning, remember that Santa, tired from his long night's work, is just returning to his village for a well-earned sleep. You might want to send a thank-you northward. Santa loves to give to others. More than anything, he loves to know that he has made your Christmas wishes come true.

Rudolph the Red-Nosed Reindeer

Rudolph is probably Santa's best-known reindeer. The smallest reindeer of them all, with a shiny red nose, poor Rudolph was teased horribly by his reindeer friends. Then one Christmas, it was so foggy and stormy that Santa thought he might not be able to deliver his gifts. Just then he noticed how Rudolph's nose lit the way in front of him. So Santa asked Rudolph, with his bright nose, to lead the reindeer team that pulled the sleigh. Rudolph safely lit Santa's way across the world so he could deliver his gifts. After that night, Rudolph wasn't teased anymore.

Gingerbread Stars

Many children around the world like to leave a jar of Christmas cookies for Santa in case he gets hungry during his hard night's work. Here's a recipe for 50 gingerbread Christmas cookies that Santa (and you!) will be sure to love.

WHAT YOU'LL NEED:

Two mixing bowls, two or three cookie sheets, plastic wrap, a rolling pin, and a star-shaped cookie cutter

INGREDIENTS:

2/3 cup softened butter

2/3 cup sugar

1/2 cup light molasses

1/4 cup milk

1 egg

3/4 cup flour

1 1/2 teaspoons baking powder

1 teaspoon ground cinnamon

1 teaspoon ground ginger

1 teaspoon ground cloves

colored sugar (for decoration)

DIRECTIONS:

1. Cream together the butter, sugar, molasses, milk, and egg in a large mixing bowl.

2. In another bowl, mix the flour, baking powder, baking soda, cinnamon, ginger, and cloves.

3. Slowly stir the flour mixture into the butter mixture, a little at a time, until the batter is creamy.

4. Turn the dough out of the bowl and wrap it in the plastic wrap.

5. Refrigerate the dough for 1 hour.

6. Preheat the oven to 350 degrees F and lightly coat two or three cookie sheets with butter.

7. After the dough has been in the refrigerator for an hour, sprinkle flour on your kitchen counter or a large cutting board. Use a rolling pin to flatten the dough to about an eighth of an inch thick.

8. Using your cookie cutter, cut the cookies out of the dough and place them on the cookie sheets. Make sure the cookies are about an inch apart.

9. Place the cookie sheets in the oven and bake for eight minutes, or until brown.

10. Using potholders, take the cookie sheets out of the oven. Decorate with colored sugar.

11. Let the stars cool.

"A Visit from Saint Nicholas"

By Clement C. Moore

'Twas the night before Christmas,
When all through the house
Not a creature was stirring, not even a
mouse;

The stockings were hung by the chimney
with care,
In hopes that St. Nicholas soon would be there;
The children were nestled all snug in their beds,
While visions of sugar-plums danced through their
heads;

And mamma in her kerchief, and I in my cap,
Had just settled our brains for a long winter's nap,—
When out on the lawn there arose such a clatter,
I sprang from my bed to see what was the matter.

Away to the window I flew like a flash,
Tore open the shutters and threw up the sash.
The moon, on the breast of the new-fallen snow,
Gave a lustre of midday to objects below;

When what to my wondering eyes should appear,
But a miniature sleigh and eight tiny reindeer,
With a little old driver, so lively and quick
I knew in a moment it must be St. Nick.

More rapid than eagles his coursers they came,
And he whistled and shouted and called them
by name;

"Now, Dasher! now, Dancer! now, Prancer
and Vixen!
On, Comet! on, Cupid! on, Donder and Blitzen!
To the top of the porch, to the top of the wall!
Now, dash away, dash away, dash away all!"

As dry leaves that before the wild hurricane fly,
When they meet with an obstacle, mount to the sky,
So, up to the housetop the coursers they flew,
With a sleigh full of toys, —and St. Nicholas too.

And then in a twinkling I heard on the roof
The prancing and pawing of each little hoof.
As I drew in my head and was turning around,
Down the chimney St. Nicholas came with a bound.

He was dressed all in fur from his head to his foot,
And his clothes were all tarnished with ashes
and soot;
A bundle of toys he had flung on his back,
And he looked like a pedlar just opening his pack.

His eyes how they twinkled! His dimples how merry!
His cheeks were like roses, his nose like a cherry;
His droll little mouth was drawn up like a bow,
And the beard on his chin was as white as the snow.

The stump of his pipe he held tight in his teeth,
And the smoke it encircled his head like a wreath.
He had a broad face, and a little round belly
That shook, when he laughed, like a bowl full
    of jelly.

He was chubby and plump, — a right jolly old elf—
And I laughed when I saw him, in spite of myself.

A wink of his eye and a twist of his head
Soon gave me to know I had nothing to dread.

He spoke not a word, but went straight to his work,
And filled all the stockings; then turned with a jerk,
And laying his finger aside of his nose.
And giving a nod, up the chimney he rose.

He sprung to his sleigh, to his team gave a whistle,
And away they all flew like the down of a thistle;
But I heard him exclaim, ere he drove out of sight:
"Happy Christmas to all, and to all a good-night!"

Your Very Own Christmas Stocking

Christmas Eve is a very special time. Santa is coming with his big bag of toys and gifts and, if you have been good, he will fill your stocking with goodies and little gifts.

Here are instructions to make your very own stocking, one that reflects who you are. You can make a ballet stocking or one that looks like a cowboy boot or any other type of shoe and decorate it any way you want to. Trace your own leg and shoe to make a newspaper pattern. If you want to make the biggest stocking you can, trace your father's shoe or the boot he wears in winter. The sewing is very easy and the decorations are put on with fabric glue.

When you go to bed on Christmas Eve, hang your stocking where Santa can see it and put a glass of milk and a plate of cookies near your stocking so he can have a snack before he and his reindeer take off for the rest of their long journey.

MATERIALS:

Newspaper for the pattern

Felt-tip pen

Scissors

1/4 yard of felt for the stocking

Straight pins

Needle

Thread

Fabric glue

Small pieces of felt in other colors for trim

Buttons for trim

1. Put on your shoe or boot. Spread the newspaper on the floor and sit down with your leg extended sideways on the newspaper. Trace around your leg and shoe with the felt-tip pen. You might want a friend to help you. If you are making the ballet slipper, point your toe. Cut out your pattern.

2. Fold the felt in half to make a double layer. Lay the pattern on the felt and pin it to both layers. With scissors, cut around the outside of the pattern, leaving about an extra ½ inch all the way around.

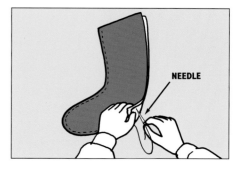

NEEDLE

3. With a needle and thread, sew along all the edges of the stocking except the top. (These are called running stitches and are the easiest sewing stitch. If you need help threading the needle ask an adult.) Be sure to leave the top of the stocking open so Santa can fill it with gifts.

4. Cut out pieces of felt for the decorations. Make any shapes you like. Using fabric glue, attach the decorations.

5. Sew buttons and ribbon trim onto top layer of felt only. Don't sew your stocking closed.

6. To make a loop so you can hang up the stocking, cut a strip of felt and fold it in half. Sew it to the top of the back layer of your stocking, near the edge or in the middle.

CHAPTER THREE

The Tradition of Gift Giving

For centuries, people have celebrated Christ's birth with gift giving. The first "gift givers" were the Magi (MA-jeye) —the three wise men who came to see the Christ Child only days after he was born. They followed a shining star to Bethlehem bearing gifts of spices and incense—frankincense, gold, and myrrh (mer)—which were worth a lot of money at the time.

Centuries later, farmers gave gifts to their workers after harvest time. And Saint Nicholas (the man many people believe to be the *real* Santa Claus) became well known for his charity and gift giving.

There are many different gift-giving traditions around the world. In Spain, children believe that the three wise men bring them gifts a week or so after Christ's birthday. In Russia, a good witch named Baboushka sneaks into houses to slip gifts under children's pillows. Swedish children have Jultomten (jule-TOME-ten), a large elf who brings them their presents, while Dutch boys and girls leave their wooden shoes by the fireside in the hope that Saint Nicholas will fill them with presents. German children place bread baskets by their front doors for the *Christkindl* (the Christ Child) to fill with cookies and candy. They believe the little boy rides from house to house on the back of a pure white donkey. They also usually leave a bundle of straw by their baskets for the donkey. And at

"The Little Drummer Boy" was one of the great gift givers of all time. You probably know the song about the poor little boy who journeyed all the way to Bethlehem to give the Christ Child the only gift he could—a song played on his snare drum. This boy showed the world that what really counts is the thought (or the sound) of the gift, not the size or cost.

The Twelve Days of Christmas

On the first day of Christmas, my true love gave to me

A partridge in a pear tree.

On the second day of Christmas my true love gave to me

Two turtledoves, and a partridge in a pear tree.

On the third day of Christmas my true love gave to me

Three French hens, two turtledoves, and a partridge in a pear tree.

On the fourth day of Christmas my true love gave to me

Four calling birds, three French hens, two turtledoves, and a partridge in a pear tree.

On the fifth day of Christmas my true love gave to me

Five Golden Rings, four calling birds, three French hens, two turtledoves, and a partridge in a pear tree.

On the sixth . . . Six geese a-laying, (repeat previous verses).

On the seventh . . . Seven swans a-swimming, (repeat previous verses).

On the eighth . . . Eight maids a-milking, (repeat previous verses).

On the ninth . . . Nine ladies dancing, (repeat previous verses).

On the tenth . . . Ten lords a-leaping, (repeat previous verses).

On the eleventh . . . Eleven pipers piping, (repeat previous verses).

German Christmas parties, a little girl often dresses up as the *Christkindl,* wearing a jeweled crown, and gives out gifts to the guests.

In England, Santa Claus is called Father Christmas. Polish children wait for someone called Star Man. In France, Père Noël brings the presents to the children on Christmas Day, but the grown-ups have to wait until New Year's Eve. Belgian children are the luckiest, though. They get their gifts on Saint Nicholas's Day—December 6!

Though getting gifts is fun, *giving* them can be even better. As Christmas approaches, do your best to think about what each member of your family would really enjoy having. Does your brother need a new baseball mitt? Maybe you can make something for your mother? Knit your sister a scarf? Or make your dad a set of note cards?

You'll have a great time wrapping each of your presents, too. There are hundreds of colorful papers you can use, or you can make your own out of newspaper or construction paper, adding fancy name tags to mark which gift goes to which person. Nothing is more exciting than the sight of the fully decorated Christmas tree surrounded by gifts in glittery packages. On Christmas morning, most families take their time and open gifts one at a time, to let the magic linger as long as possible. This way you can see the sparkle in the eye of your mother, father, or even your little brother or your big sister as she opens the present you chose just for her. And when it's your turn, don't forget to say thank you.

So this year, when you rush into the living room, ready to tear open your presents, take a moment to remember that the true spirit of Christmas is to give. Watch your families' faces as they open the gifts you give them; you'll see there what giving is all about.

On the twelfth day of Christmas my true love gave to me

Twelve drummers drumming, eleven pipers piping,

Ten lords a-leaping, nine ladies dancing,

Eight maids a-milking, seven swans a-swimming,

Six geese a-laying,

Five Golden Rings,

Four calling birds, three French hens,

Two turtledoves, and a partridge in a pear tree.

Apple Butter

Anyone can buy a gift. But how about saying "Merry Christmas" by making a friend something that looks great and is also delicious to eat? Apple butter or preserves in beautiful bottles, covered with a piece of fabric or colored cellophane and tied with ribbon, are a traditional Christmas present. Here's how to make one quart of apple butter, enough to give 4 delicious jars of preserves.

WHAT YOU'LL NEED:

A heavy saucepan, and a grater.

INGREDIENTS:

4 cups unsweetened apple sauce

1 1/2 cups packed dark brown sugar

1 teaspoon cinnamon

1/4 teaspoon allspice

pinch of ground cloves

1 lemon

DIRECTIONS:

1. Combine all the ingredients except the lemon in the heavy saucepan.

2. Cut the lemon in half and squeeze its juice into the mixture.

3. Cut away the lemon peel and rub the peel against the grater. Add the grated lemon peel to the mixture.

4. Stir the mixture

5. Cook the mixture over a low heat for approximately 4 hours, until it is thick and dark brown. Do not leave the pot unattended. Stir the mixture occasionally and be careful not to let it boil or scorch.

6. Remove the mixture from the heat and let cool.

7. Put the apple butter in a pretty jar and cover it with fabric or colored cellophane.

The Gift of the Magi

BY O. HENRY; ABRIDGED

One dollar and eighty-seven cents. That was all. And sixty cents of it was in pennies. Pennies saved one and two at a time by bullying the grocer and the vegetable man and the butcher. Three times Della counted it. One dollar and eighty-seven cents. And the next day was Christmas.

There was clearly nothing to do but flop down on the shabby little couch and howl. So Della did.

After she finished her cry and attended to her cheeks with a powder puff, Della stood by the window and looked out dully at a gray cat walking a gray fence in a gray backyard. Tomorrow would be Christmas Day, and she had only $1.87 with which to buy her husband Jim a present. She had been saving every penny she could for months, but twenty dollars a week doesn't go far and expenses had been greater than she had calculated. They always are. Many a happy hour she had spent planning for something nice for him. Something fine and rare and sterling—something just a little bit near to being worthy of the honor of being loved by Jim. Now she had only $1.87.

Now, there were two possessions of Della and Jim's in which they both took a mighty pride. One was Jim's gold watch that had been his father's and his grandfather's. The other was Della's hair. Had the Queen of Sheba lived in the flat across the airshaft, Della would have let her hair hang out the window someday to dry just to show her that her hair was more wonderful than all of Her Majesty's jewels and gifts. Had King Solomon been the janitor, with all his treasures piled up in the basement, Jim would have pulled out his watch every time he passed, just to see the king pluck at his beard from envy.

As she sat on the couch, Della undid her beautiful hair and let it fall about her, rippling and shining like a cascade of brown water. She did it up again nervously and quickly. A tear or two splashed on the worn red carpet.

Suddenly, she knew just what to do.

On went her old brown jacket; on went her old brown hat. With a whirl of skirts and with a brilliant sparkle in her eyes, she fluttered out the door and down the stairs to the street.

Where she stopped the sign read: "Mme. Sofronie. Hair Goods of All Kinds." One flight up Della ran, and collected herself, panting.

"Will you buy my hair?" asked Della.

"I buy hair," said Madame. "Take yer hat off and let's have a sight at the looks of it." Down rippled the brown cascade.

"Twenty dollars," said Madame, lifting the mass with a practiced hand.

"Give it to me quick," said Della.

Oh, and the next two hours tripped by on rosy wings. She was ransacking the stores for Jim's present.

She found it at last. It surely had been made for Jim and no one else. There was no other like it in any of the stores, and she had turned all of them inside out. It was a beautiful platinum watch chain. It was even worthy of The Watch. As soon as she

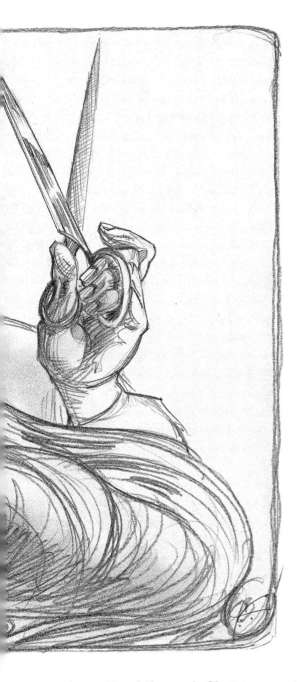

saw it she knew that it must be Jim's. It was like him. Quietness and value—the description applied to both. Twenty-one dollars they took from her for it, and she hurried home with the eighty-seven cents.

When Della reached home her happiness gave way a little to common sense. She got out her curling irons and soon her head was covered with tiny curls that made her look wonderfully like a schoolboy.

At seven o'clock, the coffee was made and the frying pan was on the back of the stove, hot and ready to cook the chops.

Jim was never late. Della doubled the watch chain in her hand and sat on the corner of the table near the door that he always entered. Then she heard his step on the stairway down on the first flight, and she turned white for just a moment. She had a habit of saying little silent prayers about the simplest everyday things, and now she whispered: "Please, God, make him think I am still pretty."

The door opened and Jim stepped in and closed it. He looked thin and very serious. Poor fellow, he was only twenty-two—and already had so much to worry about! He needed a new overcoat and he was without gloves. He looked at Della and his eyes went wide with surprise.

"Your . . . hair . . ."

Della wriggled off the table and went to him.

"Jim, darling," she cried, "don't look at me that way. I had my hair cut off and sold it because I couldn't have lived through Christmas without giving you a present. It'll grow out again—you won't mind, will you? I just had to do it. My hair grows awfully fast. Say 'Merry Christmas!' Jim, and let's be happy. You don't know what a nice—what a beautiful gift I've got for you."

Jim looked around the room curiously, looking almost shocked.

"You say your hair is gone?" he said, with an air almost of idiocy.

"You needn't look for it," said Della. "It's sold, I tell you—sold and gone, too. It's Christmas Eve, boy. Be good to me, for it went for you. Maybe the hairs of my head were numbered," she went on with sudden serious sweetness, "but nobody could ever count my love for you."

Out of his trance Jim seemed to quickly wake. He drew a package from his overcoat pocket and threw it upon the table.

"Don't make any mistake, Dell," he said, "about me. I don't think there's anything in the way of a haircut or a shave or a shampoo that could make me like my girl any less. But if you'll unwrap that package you may see why you had me going awhile at first."

White fingers and nimble tore at the string and paper. And then an ecstatic scream of joy; and then, alas! a quick change to hysterical tears and wails. Jim rushed to her side and put his arms around her.

For there lay The Combs—the set of combs that Della had worshiped for so long in a Broadway window. Beautiful combs, pure tortoiseshell, with jeweled rims—just the shade to wear in the beautiful vanished hair.

She hugged them to her bosom, and at length she was able to look up with dim eyes and a smile and say: "My hair grows so fast, Jim."

But Jim had not yet seen his beautiful present. She held it out to him eagerly upon her open palm. The dull precious metal seemed to flash with a reflection of her bright spirit.

"Isn't it a dandy, Jim? I hunted all over town to find it. You'll have to look at the time a hundred times a day now. Give me your watch. I want to see how it looks on it."

Instead of obeying, Jim tumbled down on the couch and put his hands under the back of his head and smiled.

"Dell," said he, "let's put our Christmas presents away and keep 'em awhile. They're too nice to use just at present. I sold the watch to get the money to buy your combs. And now suppose you put the chops on."

The Magi, as you know, were wise men—wonderfully wise men—who brought gifts to the Babe in the manger. They invented the art of giving Christmas presents. And here I have lamely related to you the uneventful chronicle of two foolish children who most unwisely sacrificed for each other the greatest treasures of their house. But in a last word to the wise of these days let it be said that of all who give gifts these two were the wisest. Of all who give and receive gifts, such as they, are wisest. Everywhere they are wisest. They are the Magi.

Beautiful Gift Wrapping

Make your own wrapping paper by drawing on plain paper with felt-tip pens or crayons. Add stickers and stars. Write the name of the person the gift is for on the package, too, instead of using a separate tag. The fluff of curling ribbon on the top of the gift has tiny ornaments in it and can later be hung on the Christmas tree.

MATERIALS:

White or colored tissue wrapping paper, or any other plain paper

Scissors

Tape

Felt-tip pens or crayons

Assortment of stickers

Curling ribbon for bows

Tiny ornaments

1. Wrap the package with the plain tissue paper and tape the loose ends. ***Here's how:*** Cut a piece of paper big enough to go all the way around the box, plus 3 inches extra. The paper should be extra wide to cover the ends of the box, too.

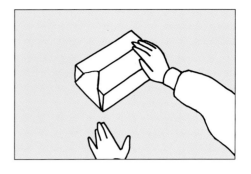

2. Wrap the paper around the box, fold under the edge an inch, and tape it in place. Then fold the paper at each end of the box to the middle to form a triangle. You may have to trim off some extra paper so the triangle folds easily.

3. Then fold the triangles up over each end of the box and tape them down.

4. Draw pictures, shapes, names, and messages on the package. Glue on stickers. Tear little scraps of tissue paper and stick them on the box.

5. Cut several long strands of ribbon in different lengths. Knot them all together at the center of the strands. Pull each strand over the scissor blade to make it curl. (Ask an adult to help you do this.) Tie a few tiny Christmas balls to the strands. Tape the cluster to the top of the box.

CHAPTER FOUR

All in the Family

Nothing draws a family closer than Christmas. Think of all the things there are to do together: choose a Christmas tree, then decorate it with bags of tinsel, strings of lights, and boxes of ornaments; make Christmas cookies; cook Christmas dinner; and more!

Now think of all the things you do *for* each other: buy or make presents; wrap them as beautifully as you can; stuff each others' stockings; bake delicious fruit cakes and pies.

Imagine this: it's Christmas Eve; the tree is lit and the fire is burning. Everyone is gathered around the piano singing Christmas carols. Your father or mother reads a poem and lights Christmas candles. Cousins and aunts and uncles and friends join the party. Even if you fight with your brothers and sisters during the rest of the year, this is a night to show how much you care about them. Before bed, your parents might let you open one present. As much as you want to see what's in the rest, you know you have to wait until morning.

But who can sleep? You're up at the crack of dawn and you wake the rest of your family. You and your brothers and sisters line up at the top of the stairs, then you run for the tree. Soon everyone is opening presents with hugs, kisses, and thank-yous all around.

Most families have their own special traditions that they carry out each year. Maybe your uncle dresses as Santa each Christmas Eve. Perhaps your grandfather reads "A Visit from Saint Nicholas." Maybe your sister plays a carol on the flute. Perhaps your dad makes a special Christmas fruit bread.

Have Yourself a Merry Little Christmas

Through the years, we all will be together

If the fates allow.

Tie a shining star above the highest bough!

And have yourself a very, merry Christmas now.

Christmas comes and goes too fast,

Fading gently to the past.

So raise a toast beneath our tree

That next year our good family

Will celebrate with hearty cheer

Another healthy, happy year.

—**Old carol, anonymous**

God bless the master of this house,

The mistress also,

And all the little children,

That round the table go,

And all your kin and kinsmen,

That dwell both far and near,

I wish you a merry Christmas

And a happy New Year.

—**Christmas carol, anonymous**

Auld Lang Syne

Should old acquaintance be forgot

And never brought to mind.

Should old acquaintance be forgot

And days of Auld Lang Syne.

For Auld Lang Syne, my dear.

For Auld Lang Syne.

We'll take a cup of kindness yet

For Auld Lang Syne.

("Auld Lang Syne" means "the good old times" in Scottish.)

The best family traditions are passed down from your grandparents to your parents to you. Just think, the Christmas traditions you observe now are the same ones your grandparents observed when they were children. Eventually, you may teach your children what your grandmother taught you to do on this special holiday.

It's the familiar traditions that make Christmas extra special. As you grow older and the years blur together, you'll always remember those "little things"—the way your family went caroling together each Christmas Eve or your great-aunt's delicious homemade cookies.

These are memories you and your family will share for years to come. They are also traditions that you can continue and, one day, pass on to your own children.

The first family Christmas ever was spent in a stable, with Mary, Joseph, and the baby Jesus in a manger. It is said that a cow blew gently on Jesus to keep him warm, and that a sheep gave his wool so that Mary could weave her child a warm blanket.

Sending Christmas cards is a wonderful tradition that keeps you in touch with old friends. This year (along with your letter to Santa), make a list of people you want to send good cheer to, and write them a holiday greeting. You can either buy cards in the store, or if you're feeling creative, make your own.

Some Italian families fast all of Christmas Day! Then, after a midnight mass, they sit down to a gigantic feast. Being hungry for an entire day must certainly draw a family closer together and make them appreciate the food they have.

Mini Pizza

Mini pizzas are something your whole family can make and—even better—eat together. You can put whatever toppings you want on your pizza: mushrooms, pepperoni, peppers. Some people even like unusual things like pineapple. You can also use pieces of pepperoni and mushrooms to decorate your pizza the way you like; two pieces of pepperoni as eyes, a mushroom for a nose, and a pepper for a mouth can make a good face. Use your imagination to make a delicious and artistic meal.

There are a few different steps to making a good pizza. Why not assign a different task to each member of your family? Perhaps Dad can spread on the tomato sauce. Your brother or sister can spread on the cheese. Get your family lined up in a row and start making pizza!

INGREDIENTS:

8 pita breads

2 14-ounce jars tomato sauce

Spices: basil, oregano, garlic powder

4 cups grated mozzarella cheese

Toppings: pepperoni, peppers, onions, mushrooms, and whatever else you like

DIRECTIONS:

1. Toast pitas.

2. Spread tomato sauce evenly over each pita.

3. Sprinkle on spices.

4. Sprinkle mozzarella cheese over the pizza so the entire pita covered with cheese.

5. Decorate your pizza with toppings.

6. Put the pizzas in the broiler for about four minutes or until the cheese melts and begins to brown.

A Most Unusual Family Holiday

The doorbell! Hal threw down his pen and went to the door. Interruptions! He'd never finish writing his legal brief. The City Dog Pound was suing Mrs. Hanning's Home for Stray Cats—a very important case. He was due in court in two weeks, only two days after Christmas!

"Who is it?" Hal asked through the door.

"Mailman, sir . . ."

Hal opened the door and blinked.

"What? What is it?"

The mailman smiled. "Appears to be a tree of some sort." It was true. A small tree with young fruit hanging from the branches was standing on the front porch. "This came with it, too," the mailman went on, and pulled a bird cage from out of his mailbag.

"A . . . bird?" Hal blinked again. "Who in the world . . ."

The mailman handed him a pink envelope. "There's a note, sir."

Hal tore it open. The message was simple, in elegant blue script:

"For the first day of Christmas, from your true loves, Jane, Stevie, and Angela."

Hal shook his head and smiled. As in the song "The Twelve Days of Christmas," his wife, Jane, and children, Stevie, age five, and Angela, three, had sent him a partridge and a pear tree.

He smiled at the mailman. "Thank you, sir."

Hal spent the rest of the morning planting the tree in the front yard, then went to the store to purchase bird feed.

"They're beautiful," Hal told Jane that night over the phone.

"I'm glad, dear." Then she paused. "So when do you think you can join us here at Mother's? It's wonderful, but we miss you."

Hal sighed. "Honey," he said, "you know I'd like to come right now, but I've got work."

"Well, it *is* two weeks before Christmas," his wife said.

In the background, Hal could hear his children playing.

"I know," he replied. "I'll try to finish this brief as fast as I can. Give my love to the kids."

The next morning, the doorbell rang at about the same time. Again, Hal stood up from his desk in a huff.

"Yes?" he demanded.

"Mailman, sir."

Hal swung the door open. This time the man in blue handed over two beautiful turtledoves (each in a separate cage), pure white and cooing gently.

"There's another note, sir," the mailman said with a wry smile.

"For the second day of Christmas, from your true loves, Jane, Stevie, and Angela."

Hal shook his head. *Doves?* What did he need with doves! A partridge in a pear tree was one thing, but doves? Christmas—what an inconvenient holiday—always interrupting his work! Grumbling, he hung the cages in the living room and went right back to his desk.

The next three mornings each brought a new delivery along with the same note: "From your true loves."

Hal was now host to three French hens that ran wildly around his backyard, four calling birds, whose calling schedule was usually somewhere between one and three in the morning, and five golden rings the size of Hula Hoops.

When the mailman carried in six geese a-laying on the morning of the sixth day, Hal was occupied feeding animals while trying not to step on eggs and had not yet made it to his desk.

"Jane," he raged that night into the phone. "You and the kids have taken this Christmas joke too far!"

"Joke?" Jane said. "This is no joke."

Just then, Angela, his three-year-old, picked up on the other extension. "How do you like our presents, Daddy?"

Hal clenched his teeth. "They're beautiful, sweetheart."

The next four days the doorbell rang at the same time.

Bzzz!

Hal put the seven swans a-swimming in the bathtub. He invited the eight maids a-milking (complete with cows) to find their own spots in the backyard. He pushed the nine ladies dancing into the guest room. Hal didn't know quite where to put the ten lords a-leaping, so they leaped as they would, often over his desk during the few spare moments when he wasn't feeding swans, doves, hens, the partridge, or trying not to break eggs.

At least the cows are outside, he thought to himself, but soon jugs of milk were spilling out of the refrigerator onto the kitchen floor.

The piping pipers brought the first in a series of complaints from neighbors and the drumming of the twelve drummers brought a summons from the police. Well, thought Hal, fuming, Jane and the kids may be my true loves, but enough is enough! This is *not* my idea of a merry Christmas! He grabbed the unfinished brief, shoved it in his suitcase, and ran off to his meeting with Mrs. Hanning and her cats.

That night, Jane, Stevie, and Angela came home.

"Jane!" Hal shouted as she came in the house. "This is crazy! My ears are ringing! My fingers shake! My . . ."

Just then a leaping lord did a triple-spin pirouette over the sofa. Hal shook his head.

"Jane, I love you, but please."

Hal's true love was laughing.

"Isn't it wonderful?" she said, her eyes bright. "Hal, don't you see—tomorrow is Christmas and we have a wonderful group of people, not to mention creatures, to spend it with!"

Hal opened his mouth to speak, but no words came. His shoulders relaxed as he looked around the room. The hens, the geese, the lords, the dancing ladies—what a group! Even though they had made a ruins of the house, the chaos suddenly seemed absolutely wonderful. Glancing outside, he saw the eight maids milking away. The thin trace of a smile spread over his face and grew until he was laughing. He threw his pen over his shoulder and opened his arms to his wife and children.

"Well," he said, with a broad grin, "I guess Mrs. Hanning's Home for Stray Cats can wait." He hugged his family to him. "Merry Christmas!"

As Hal, Jane, and the children grew old they invited, every lord, maid, and goose each year for Christmas dinner. Angela loved playing with the swans, and Stevie turned out to be quite a fine leaper himself.

And though they might have gotten some strange looks from the neighbors, everyone certainly agreed that they were a family who really knew how to enjoy a holiday.

Partridges for Your Pear Tree

May these glittering partridges alight on your Christmas tree. The whole family of birds is made from pinecones, pompons, and feathers. Depending on the kinds of pinecones you have, you can make big, medium, or tiny partridges or some of each, like a family.

MATERIALS:

MAKES ONE PARTRIDGE:

1 white pompon (for the head)

1 pinecone

Tiny pieces of black and brown felt

2 big or 4 to 6 small feathers (for wings)

1 foot of gold cord

Scissors

Craft glue

Gold glitter

1. Cut out tiny black eyes from felt, and glue them on the pompon. Cut out a brown triangle for the beak. Fold it in half and glue it to the pompon. Glue the head on the fat end of the pinecone near the top edge.

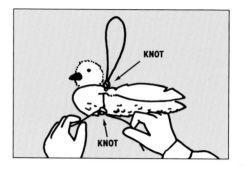

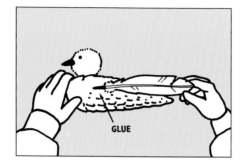

2. Select one big feather or a bunch of little feathers for each wing. Put a drop of glue on the quill end of each feather and slip it between the branches of the pinecone near the middle of the cone.

3. Fold the gold cord in half, then tie a knot about halfway to form a loop. Wrap the two loose ends of the cord around the pinecone just behind the wings and tie them loosely.

4. Hold the bird by the cord to make sure it doesn't hang lopsided. Move the cord forward or back on the cone if necessary. Then knot the ends tightly around the pinecone.

5. Spread glue on the top edges of the pinecone, at the base of the wings, and on the head. Sprinkle on the gold glitter. It helps to lay a piece of paper under the partridge before you sprinkle the glitter. It is then easy to shake off the excess glitter and pour it back into its container.

CHAPTER FIVE

Christmas Carols

Silent Night!, Holy Night!
All is calm, All is bright.

As soon as Thanksgiving week ends, the familiar, warm sounds of Christmas carols begin to fill the air. No other holiday has inspired as many magical melodies: "Joy to the World," "God Bless Ye Merry Gentlemen," "The Holly and the Ivy"—the list goes on and on. As Christmas Day approaches, the songs are played more and more frequently. You might sing "The Twelve Days of Christmas" as you trim the tree, or find yourself humming "Oh, Little Town of Bethlehem," as you shop for gifts, each and every note adding to the excitement and magic of the season.

On Christmas Eve many families go to church and sing in beautiful harmony with the choir and the rest of the congregation. Then at home, the music making continues. Someone in your family pulls out old, faded sheet music, and you gather around the piano and enjoy song after song. Or you can put some music on the stereo and sing along.

Many times, groups of carolers stroll snowy streets and knock on neighbor's doors. Sometimes they are invited in for a warm drink of hot chocolate and cookies.

Portugal has a wonderful caroling tradition. The carolers wait until well after dark, then go to the neighbors, gather outside a window, and strum guitars and sing. The neighbors wake up, throw on warm clothes, join the singers, and go on to the next house. And so it goes, until nearly the entire neighborhood is out singing. Then, after celebrating together, everyone goes home, exhausted, but full of good cheer.

We Wish You A Merry Christmas

We wish you a merry Christmas,
We wish you a merry Christmas,
We wish you a merry Christmas,
And a happy new year!

Good tidings we bring,
To you and your kin.
We wish you a merry Christmas,
And a happy new year!

Joy to the World

Joy to the world, the Lord has come.

Let Earth receive her king.

Let every heart prepare Him room.

And Heaven and Nature sing!

And Heaven and Nature sing!

And Heaven and Nature sing!

A Bedtime Carol

At bedtime when I cannot sleep I count
　　my sheep—my special sheep.

The first I count is the one that lay

close to the Christ child on the hay

and kept him warm that Christmas Day.

O Little Town of Bethlehem

O little town of Bethlehem,

How still we see thee lie!

Above thy deep and dreamless sleep

Thy silent stars go by.

Yet in thy dark streets shineth the
　　everlasting light;

The hopes and fears of all the years

Are met in thee tonight.

An old tradition in Italy goes like this: men with tiny flutes and wood recorders come down from the hills on Christmas Eve and roam the town, piping music to honor the birth of Jesus.

No one knows who wrote most of the great Christmas carols. Many have been passed from generation to generation, and all celebrate the wonderful traditions of Christmas. There's "Good King Wenceslaus," about the kind king who shared his Christmas feast with a poor peasant he saw from his window. No one knows who wrote "The Twelve Days of Christmas," either, but can you imagine a Christmas season without at least once singing about the partridge in a pear tree or five golden rings?

Of course there are many famous Christmas songs, such as "Rudolph the Red-Nosed Reindeer," "Winter Wonderland," and "Frosty the Snowman," that have been written within the last fifty years. These songs have become as much of the holiday as the traditional carols.

Most families have recordings of Christmas carols and songs. As soon as these are put on the record player, the mood of the house changes—nothing brings back warm memories of good times more than music.

So don't be shy this year. When the Christmas carolers come by your house, sing with them as loud as you can. Christmas carols are for everyone to share. It doesn't matter if you sing off-key or you don't know all the words, just sing out and enjoy!

Most Christmas carols were written by religious men who wanted to celebrate Christ's birth through the warmth of song. In the early 1800s, Davies Gilbert and William Sandys published a book of forgotten carols including: "The First Nowell," "I Saw Three Ships," and "God Rest Ye Merry Gentlemen." This publication allowed many great Christmas carols you love today to be passed on through the generations.

In 1865, Phillip Brooks, a bishop from Massachusetts, visited the Holy Land. Three years later he remembered his trip and wrote the words to the well-known carol "O Little Town of Bethlehem." His church's organist, Lewis Redner, wrote the tune and since then, the song has remained one of the world's best-loved carols.

Hot Chocolate

This year, invite Christmas carolers into your home and offer them something hot to drink, to warm them up and soothe their throats. Here's an easy way to make a quart of hot chocolate from scratch.

WHAT YOU'LL NEED:

A medium-sized saucepan, an egg beater

INGREDIENTS:

1/3 cup unsweetened cocoa or white chocolate

1/2 cup sugar

Dash of salt

1/3 cup water

1 quart milk

3/4 teaspoon vanilla

DIRECTIONS:

1. Combine the unsweetened cocoa (or white chocolate), sugar, and salt in the saucepan.

2. Blend in water and bring the mixture to a boil over medium heat, stirring constantly. This should take about two minutes.

3. After the mixture is boiling, turn the heat down very low and add the milk. Stir until hot, but DO NOT BOIL.

4. Remove the mixture from the heat and add the vanilla, then beat it lightly with an egg beater.

5. Add whipped cream, marshmallows, or cinnamon sticks.

The Christmas Concert

Miss Handleman, the choir director, stomped forward.

"I'm very, very sorry," she said. "But some of you simply aren't getting it. I hate to single people out, but the Christmas concert is tomorrow and a few of you keep singing flat!"

The choir, a collection of boys and girls, shifted uneasily. Miss Handleman's fierce gaze turned on Wayne.

"I'm very sorry," Miss Handleman said, sternly. "But when we come to the high part of 'White Christmas,' just mouth the words." She smiled. "That tenor line must be pure and smooth, flowing gently like a river, not belted out like . . . like some sort of sick bird!"

Wayne felt his face go completely red. His heart sank to the pit of his stomach.

"We are performing music by *Mozart! Brahms!*" Miss Handleman thundered, waving her arms wildly. "As well as many other favorites! Some of the world's great composers. Now, please." She rapped her baton. "From the top, shall we?"

On the way home from school, Jim put his arm around his friend's shoulder.

"Don't worry about Miss Handleman. She's a loon. You know, nervous. The principal and all the parents will be at the concert. She's probably worried she'll be fired or something if we don't sound just perfect."

Wayne frowned and forced a smile. "I guess . . ." He sighed. "Well, who wants to be a great rock star, anyway."

Jim smiled. "Rock?" Jim asked. "You?"

Wayne shrugged. "I've never told anyone, but . . ." He sighed. "It's just a stupid dream of mine."

Jim sighed. "You never know, Wayne."

Wayne forced a smile. "Yeah, well, I'd better run."

The friends parted and just as Wayne rounded the corner, out of the brush appeared a scraggly man with a gray beard and a bright red crew cut.

"Trouble singin' on key, heh?" he said, exposing a set of fully plated gold teeth. "Trouble with the old vocal cords? That's what the buzz is around my neck of the woods."

Wayne took a step back. The man stepped forward. Who was he? The man grinned

wildly and giggled like a mad elf.

"Oh, yes, sonny boy, high notes are difficult, sure enough, but here!"

The man shoved a brown paper bag into Wayne's hand.

"You listen to me. I know you want to sing the high tenor line. No! Don't deny it—of course, you do. Show up that old hag of a choir director. She's more concerned about making a perfect sound for the principal than making sure everyone has fun. That's not Christmas spirit, in my thinkin'!"

The man's green eyes sparkled. He pointed a finger toward the bag.

"Eat these magic specks before the concert! Look at 'em. That's right! See how they glitter and pop and jump and dance!" Here the man giggled again and his eyes flashed.

"Ohh! Something wonderful will happen to you! Something absolutely wonderful!"

Wayne felt a shiver. Wide-eyed, he looked into the bag. When he looked up again, the man was gone.

"You're in a quiet mood today," Wayne's father said at dinner. "Ready for tomorrow's concert?"

Wayne's heart was pounding. Should he tell his parents about the strange little man and the green specks? Should he tell his parents that Miss Handleman told him not to sing the high tenor part?

"I guess I am . . ." Then he smiled. "Yeah, Dad. I think we'll sound great!"

The auditorium was jam-packed the next evening. Parents, teachers, and students filled every seat. Folding chairs were set up in the back to accommodate the large crowd. As Wayne took his place on the stage, his palms were sweaty, his heart thumping.

Miss Handleman stood to the side, hunched over the music, her face pale even with the heavy makeup.

The room hushed as Mr. Rittle, the school principal, a large man with a handlebar mustache, strode to the podium.

"Welcome to our annual Christmas concert," he began, in a full, robust voice. "As usual, Miss Handleman has done a fabulous job of preparing these boys and girls to sing for you tonight." Miss Handleman blushed. "And now," the principal went on, "without further ado. . . let the show begin!"

The audience applauded politely as Miss Handleman stepped toward the stage. Jim nudged Wayne.

"Hey," he whispered. "Why're you grinning? I didn't even think you'd show up after how Miss Handleman embarrassed you yesterday."

Wayne fingered the bag in his pocket. "I don't know . . . I just got the Christmas spirit, I guess."

"We shall begin," Miss Handleman told the audience, "with 'The Holly and the Ivy.'"

She raised her arms and the choir started softly, beautifully. When the piece was done the crowd applauded politely. Wayne could barely concentrate. He noticed his parents beaming at him. Should he take the green specks? What would happen if he did? Would he sing better? Maybe he'd sing worse. . . .

The chorus sang one number, then the next, each song greeted with mild applause, until it was time for the final number: "White Christmas."

Raising her baton, Miss Handleman peered at Wayne and mouthed, "Don't sing." Wayne narrowed his eyes. Rage burned within him. In a flash, he reached into the bag, grabbed the pellets in his fist and swallowed every one.

Miss Handleman brought down her arms and the choir began. At first Wayne felt nothing, but then, halfway through the song, he felt a thump in his stomach . . . and then a wild surge of energy. The choir was singing quietly: "I'm dreaming of a white Christmas!"

But not Wayne. He sang like he always dreamed he could—all out and with rhythm.

Jim looked at him wide-eyed. "What are you doing?" he whispered.

But it was too late.

"Just like the ones I used to know!" Wayne sang out.

Miss Handleman's face turned red, so angry that she didn't even realize that Wayne was singing perfectly on pitch. "Wayne!" she hissed.

Wayne started to clap his hands and walked down the platform toward the audience. "Where the treetops glisten! And children listen!"

At first the audience rustled uneasily in their seats. But then, they suddenly began to clap their hands. Miss Handleman looked over her shoulder. Everyone was smiling. And now the choir, picking up on Wayne's cue, began to sway back and forth.

"To hear sleigh bells in the snow!"

"Wayne!" Miss Handleman demanded. "Stop at once!"

But there was no stopping the feeling in the room. Wayne was down on one knee, singing with all his heart, hitting every note, high and low, right on the nose. Just then, Mr. Rittle strutted across the stage, shouting out the words. Miss Handleman looked around her. A somber Christmas concert had suddenly turned into something joyous. Everyone around the room was clapping, dancing, moving, smiling. Wayne sang out in beautiful tenor, "I'm dreaming of a white Christmas! With every Christmas card I write!"

Wayne's parents were beaming. The next thing Miss Handleman knew, Mr. Rittle was dancing with her across the stage. Wayne stepped center stage and smiled at his parents as he sang out the final chorus. The audience rose to its feet and cheered. Suddenly,

the scraggly man jumped onstage, beaming.

"Wow!" Wayne shouted. "Those green specks sure worked some kind of magic!" The man winked at Wayne. "There was no magic in those specks." He did a double flip, landed on his feet, and grinned wildly. "Just a little trick I played to get you to believe in yourself. Not to mention to get everyone in this concert hall into the right kind of Christmas spirit!"

Flabbergasted, Wayne felt Miss Handleman and Mr. Rittle put their arms around his shoulders.

"Encore!" someone cried.

"Excellent idea!" Mr. Rittle said.

And together, Wayne, Miss Handleman, and Mr. Rittle led the audience through another rousing chorus: "May your days be sunny and bright! And may all your Christmases be white!"

A Christmas Songbook

Make a songbook you can use every Christmas. Copy the words to your favorite carols and decorate the pages, too. You could make a book for each member of your family, and personalize it with a name or initials so everyone can sing along. The cover is made of wrapping paper decorated with paper cutouts, and the inside pages are colored construction paper.

MATERIALS:

5 or 6 9 x 12 inch sheets construction paper

Sharp embroidery needle or a large sharp needle

Cotton embroidery floss

Scissors

2 8 1/2 x 11 inch pieces of cardboard

1 piece wrapping paper (for the cover)

Glue stick

2-inch-wide fabric tape (for the binding)

Scraps of patterned wrapping paper (for cutouts)

Alphabet stickers (for the title)

Colored felt-tip pens

1. Layer sheets of construction paper, then fold them in half.

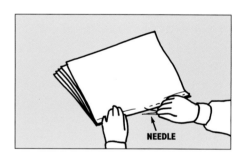

2. Thread the needle with floss. Double the floss and knot the end. Sew through all the sheets of construction paper on the fold. Use the running stitch.

3. Lay the pages on one piece of cardboard with the fold line even with one edge. Trace around the paper. With the ruler, draw lines on the cardboard ½ inch outside the traced line. Cut along the outside lines. Repeat with the other piece of cardboard.

4. Lay one piece of cardboard on the wrong side of the wrapping paper and trace around it. Then measure 2 inches away from this line and draw another line. Cut along the outside line. Repeat with the other piece of cardboard.

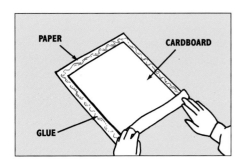

5. Lay the cardboard along the traced line, then spread glue along the edges on the wrong side of the paper. Fold the extra paper onto the cardboard and glue it down, starting with the corners. Cover the other piece of cardboard the same way.

6. Cut another strip of cardboard about ¼ inch wide and the same height as the covers. This is the spine of the book.

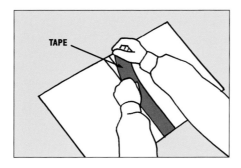

7. Lay the front and back covers wrong sides facing you. Lay the cardboard spine in between them. Cut a piece of tape the same height as the covers and lay it down so it covers the edges of each cover with the spine in the center. Trim the ends of the tape flush with the edge of the cover.

8. Turn the cover over. Cut another piece of tape 3 inches longer than the cover and center it along the spine. Fold the ends to the inside of the cover.

9. Write your favorite songs on the pages but leave the first and last pages blank. These will be glued to the inside of the cardboard cover. Decorate the pages with wrapping paper cutouts or stickers.

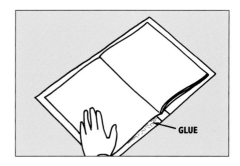

10. To assemble the book, spread glue on the inside of the front cover. Glue the first page to it. Then spread glue on the inside of the back cover and glue down the last page.

11. Decorate the front cover with cutouts and use stick-on letters to write your own title.

CHAPTER SIX

The Joy of Sharing

Christmas is a holiday that celebrates love, giving, and sharing. Jesus preached: "Do unto others as you would have them do unto you." Saint Nicholas, the man many suspect to be the real Santa Claus, was known for his charitable deeds.

In fact, when Saint Nick was only twelve, a terrible plague killed both of his parents. Rather than live off his inheritance, Nicholas gave over half the money his parents left him to charity and used the rest to put himself through school. Nicholas was ordained a priest at the young age of nineteen, at the same time the Roman emperor Diocletian (deye-oh-CLEE-shun) came into power. Diocletian decreed that all his citizens worship him as a god. Nicholas refused and was thrown in jail for five years. Nicholas's time in prison strengthened his faith. Upon his release, he devoted his life to helping others. For this he was made a saint.

There are some stories that illustrate Nicholas's generosity. One tale tells how Saint Nicholas saved a merchant and his three lovely daughters. The merchant, once very rich, had lost all his money. Every cent was gone and he was in an absolutely hopeless state. But Saint Nicholas came to the rescue, mysteriously delivering a bag of gold to the family. A month or so later, he did it again and this time the merchant chased Nicholas through the streets to thank him for saving his family from a life of poverty. Saint Nicholas smiled and made the man promise to never tell who had helped him. It was only on the man's deathbed that he revealed Nicholas's good deed.

Of all the joys a man can feel
The joys that are most rare
Are the times that he can reach
Into his heart and share.

—OLD CAROL

For Them

Before you bid, for Christmas' sake,
Your guests to sit at meat,
Oh please to save a little cake
For them that have no treat.

Before you go down party-dressed
In silver gown or gold,
Oh please to send a little vest
To them that still go cold.

Before you give your girl and boy
Gay gifts to be undone,
Oh please to spare a little toy
To them that will have none.

Before you gather round the tree
To dance the day about,
Oh please to give a little glee
To them that go without.

—Eleanor Farjeon

"A merry Christmas, Bob!" said Scrooge, with an earnestness that could not be mistaken, as he clapped him on the back. "A merrier Christmas, Bob, my good fellow, than I have given you for many a year! I'll raise your salary and endeavor to assist your struggling family, and we will discuss your affairs this very afternoon over a Christmas bowl of smoking bishop, Bob! Make up the fires and buy another coal scuttle before you dot another i, Bob Cratchit!"

—Charles Dickens, *A Christmas Carol*

There is one other version of this tale: the three lovely daughters hung their wet stockings by the fire then went to bed. In the middle of the night, Nicholas snuck into the house and filled them with gold. (This legend began the tradition of hanging stockings by the fireplace.)

By all accounts, Saint Nicholas was a remarkably generous man. Now, it's certainly not necessary to give away sacks of gold, but this Christmas, maybe you could give away that extra pair of shoes you have, or bake your favorite cake for a relief organization, or perhaps even spend a day collecting money for the poor. Many towns have "food banks" that accept donations of canned goods for the needy. Perhaps you could help in a soup kitchen or at a homeless shelter.

There are so many things to give: stuffed animals, toys, books to less fortunate children—anything that you think would give someone else pleasure. Many families clean out their closets and donate clothes that are too small (or sometimes nice ones that fit!) to the poor. Never forget: what may be too small for you may fit someone else perfectly. So before you throw anything out, think about giving it away.

Of course, everyone should be as generous as possible every day of their lives, but Christmas is a time to think not only of family and friends, but of all of those in the world who are less fortunate, those who may not be lucky enough to sit down to a satisfying Christmas dinner.

Remembering the needy and, more important, helping them are what Christmas is really all about.

Kwanzaa (KWAHN-zah) is an African-American celebration, a time for family to be together. The holiday lasts from December 26 to 31. During this time, everyone fasts to cleanse the body and soul. On the evening of the thirty-first, they gather around a karamu (kah-RAH-mu) table for a feast and share their food with neighbors and friends, just as their ancestors shared food from the hunt and harvest.

Did you know there was an army whose uniforms were Santa Claus suits? Well, it's true—the Salvation Army is an organization that collects money for the poor every Christmas. Just look for the Santa on your town's main street, ringing a bell.

Muffin Mania

Sharing with others is one of the great joys of the Christmas season. A muffin party is the perfect way to share good food and good feelings.

Gather with friends at someone's home. Each of you bring your favorite muffin ingredient—blueberry, cranberry, pecans, dates, chocolate chips, or anything else that sounds tasty.

Follow the recipe below to make a batch of plain muffin mix. Then you should each add your favorite muffin ingredient to your part of the mix.

Share your muffins with your friends, and they'll share their muffins with you! You can also make a batch to give away.

WHAT YOU'LL NEED FOR EACH BATCH OF 12 MUFFINS:

Buttered muffin pans, a large mixing bowl, a small bowl, and a toothpick.

INGREDIENTS:

2 cups white flour

3 teaspoons baking powder

1/2 teaspoon salt

2 tablespoons sugar

1 egg

1 cup milk

1/4 cup melted butter

ADD-INS: cranberries, blueberries, walnuts, pecans, dates, raisins, chocolate chips

DIRECTIONS:

1. Preheat the oven to 375 degrees F.

2. Mix the flour, baking powder, salt, and sugar in the mixing bowl.

3. Break the egg into the small bowl and beat it slightly. Now add the egg, milk, and butter to the flour mixture, stirring only enough to dampen the flour. IMPORTANT: The batter should not be completely smooth. It should be a little bit lumpy.

4. Add your favorite muffin ingredient. If you are adding fruit, add 1 cup of fruit and ½ cup sugar to the batter. If you are adding nuts, add ½ cup nuts and ¼ cup sugar to the batter. If adding dates, add ½ cup of dates and no sugar. If adding raisins, add ⅓ cup of raisins and no sugar.

5. Spoon the batter into the muffin pans, filling each cup about two-thirds full.

6. Bake for 20 to 25 minutes, until a toothpick inserted into the center comes out clean.

7. Using potholders, take muffins out of the oven and let them cool.

Good King Wenceslaus

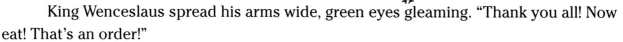

 It was a cold, bitter Christmas Eve, but inside the royal palace, King Wenceslaus—known far and wide as "Good King Wenceslaus"—sat before a banquet table brimming with food.

"Roast turkey, sire?" his first attendant asked.

King Wenceslaus tugged on his beard and smiled.

"But of course! Roast turkey! And stuffing! And gravy! Oh, give me the works! But not just me! Come! Everyone! Join the feast! Eat! Eat!"

The first attendant served the turkey, a second covered it with gravy, a duke added a dab of cranberry sauce, and an earl scooped on some string beans.

"Your food, Your Highness!" the earl announced.

King Wenceslaus spread his arms wide, green eyes gleaming. "Thank you all! Now eat! That's an order!"

So the feast began. The queen, earl, duke, attendants, and assorted lords heaped their plates high. As they ate, the court minstrels sang and then the court jester told jokes and juggled.

"A toast!" the first attendant cried halfway through the meal. "To King Wenceslaus! The best of all kings! The kindest ruler ever!"

The king blushed. "Now, let's not go overboard . . . ."

"Oh, but if anything, I understate the case," the first attendant replied. "What other king in the history of the world has passed laws outlawing hunger! In Good King Wenceslaus's rule, never has a subject in his realm gone hungry!"

"It's true!" a duke shouted.

"A certified fact!" the court statistician said, pulling out a series of graphs and charts. "It's all fully documented!"

"What a man!" stated the earl.

"A *goodly* man!" the queen asserted.

Cries echoed around the room: "Speech! Speech!"

Good King Wenceslaus exchanged an embarrassed glance with his wife.

"Go on," she said, nudging him. "Say a few words. You deserve it, dearest."

"Oh . . . all right . . ." The king stood, raising a brass goblet. "Ah, Christmas Eve! What a joyous night! A night for sharing! First, I must thank my chief assistants who have helped me institute my five-year plan to eliminate all forms of hunger from the land. Without their loyal help, I might . . ."

But suddenly, the king's voice broke. There were murmurs around the table.

"Are you all right, sire?" the earl asked.

But King Wenceslaus didn't answer. Instead, he moved toward the corner window, his face with a blank expression.

"What's wrong with the king?" someone asked, concerned.

"Fetch a doctor! Quickly!"

But the king raised his hand for silence and pressed his nose to the windowpane. Outside he saw a man, wearing only a light cloak, mittenless, scrounging in the snow for firewood. The king's beard drooped. His sparkly green eyes grew dull.

"There's a man outside," he said, his voice aquiver. "A . . . a poor peasant . . ."

"A peasant?" the earl said with a laugh. "Surely you're seeing things!"

"A figment of your brilliant kingly imagination!" offered the duke.

But the queen came to her husband's side. "Show him to me, dearest," she urged.

The king raised a finger and the queen looked just in time to see the peasant grab a wet piece of firewood and disappear into the darkness.

"He must be so cold, out on such a night!" the king said, then spun around to face the room. His eyes widened. "How can we sit here in warmth and comfort with food in our bellies, while he, poor soul, is so cold that he must scrounge for wood—on Christmas Eve, no less!"

"But, Your Highness, perhaps things aren't as bad for the man as they seem. . . ."

"Pack up a bundle of food!" the king bellowed. "The best from our royal feast! All the leftovers! And gather up some firewood. Dry firewood!"

For an instant, nobody moved. Then the duke nodded.

"Our good king is sending an errand boy to give that poor peasant a good Christmas meal," he cried.

"An errand boy?" the king bellowed, his brows furrowed. "No! I shall go myself!"

"But, Your Majesty! The weather . . . it's *cold* out there."

The king ignored all protests. "Who'll come with me? Who?"

A meek voice from the back of the room piped up. "I . . . I will, Your Majesty."

A small page boy, no more than twelve years old, stepped forward. A few years earlier, the king had found this boy, Ethan, living half-starved in the city streets and had brought him into his court. If anyone knew firsthand of life's hardships, it was Ethan, and he was always there, ready to help others. King Wenceslaus smiled broadly.

"Excellent, my son! I'll be honored by your company. Now let's get moving! Pack a feast fit for a king!"

Everywhere in the room, people worked to gather food and dry wood. Soon the king, with an enormous sack of food over his shoulder and the young page, carrying the firewood, whisked out of the banquet hall.

It was bitter and snowy—the kind of night even a polar bear would avoid. But the weather seemed to cheer the king.

"Come, Ethan," he shouted into the howling wind. "We must hurry, or the peasant's tracks will be covered."

The king marched forward. After a time, he began to whistle and the boy, doing his best to keep up in the ankle-deep snow, sang along, too.

"It does the heart good to be out on such an errand!" the king said.

The boy nodded. "That it does, Your Majesty. Thank you so for . . . for letting me come along."

"Nonsense!" the king replied with a wave of his hand. "Thank you for the help . . . and the company. Now we'd better hurry!"

By now the last glimmer of sunlight had dipped under the horizon. The king, with a lantern to light the way in one hand, strode forward. But the page, a thin boy, had trouble keeping pace.

At the top of the hill, the king stopped and waited for the boy to catch up. "Hey there . . .," the king asked, concerned. "Are you all right? Why . . . you're shivering. "

"It's nothing serious, Your Majesty." Ethan's teeth chattered.

"Nothing serious? It's most serious! Here, take my cloak."

The page's eyes widened. "Your Majesty's cloak . . . . I . . . I couldn't. I can't! I won't!"

But the king had already draped the heavy cloak over Ethan's shoulders. He patted the page on the back. "Just follow directly behind me, my boy. I'll block out these cold winds, and we'll give that poor peasant a Christmas he'll never forget."

"How was it?" the queen asked late that night, when her husband had returned.

The king smiled. "At first the peasant didn't really believe it was me! But I convinced him soon enough. And after he and his family ate, Ethan sang some carols. He has a beautiful tenor voice. And the peasant's daughter did a delightful dance." The king shook his head, satisfied. "It was a Christmas to remember. Sharing the kingly feast with a needy peasant family—that's what Christmas is all about, isn't it?"

"What, dear?" the queen asked.

The king smiled. "Sharing, my darling. Sharing."

With those words, he blew out his lantern and fell into a deep, satisfied (not to mention goodly) sleep.

A Snowman Cookie Jar

Let Frosty the Snowman greet Santa with a jar full of cookies on Christmas Eve. A hot cup of cocoa will warm him up and help him get through his long night of work. Frosty is made from a canning jar, a tube sock, and some trimmings.

MATERIALS:

A tube sock with striped ribbing

Scissors

Polyester fiberfill for stuffing (enough to fill a softball)

Thread

Needle

Red pompons for hat and buttons

Orange felt for carrot nose, black felt for eyes and mouth, red felt for scarf

Strong rubber band

Paper hole punch

Craft glue

1. Cut tube sock in half between the ribbing and the toe, leaving the toe end for the head and the ribbing end for the hat. Stuff the toe with fiberfill to make the head, leaving about 5 inches for the neck and collar.

2. Gather the sock at the base of the head, sew a few stitches to hold it in place, and then wrap the thread around the base several times and knot it.

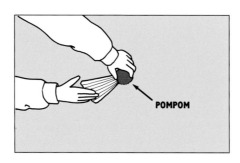

POMPOM

3. To make the hat, turn the ribbed end of the sock inside out, gather the cut end and with needle and thread sew it shut. Turn it right side out and glue a red pompon at the sewn tip.

4. Cut a small triangle of orange felt, spread glue along one edge, and roll the triangle into a cone or carrot for the nose. To glue the nose to the head, spread a thin row of glue around the base and stick it on the face.

5. Decorate the face with black felt eyes. Cut the dots using the paper hole punch and glue them under the nose for the mouth. Cut a long strip of red felt for the scarf, and cut fringe on each end.

RUBBER BAND

6. Slip a rubber band around the neck (the part of the sock that is open under the head) and stretch the neck over the top of the jar. You may need help to hold the head in place and to pull the neck part down. Slip the rubber band down over the lid of the jar so that it holds the neck in place. There is a groove around the top of the lid and the rubber

band will fit snugly once it is in this groove. Roll the excess neck fabric back up over the rubber band to cover it and form a turtleneck shirt for the snowman.

7. Glue red pompons to the front of the jar for buttons. Put on Frosty's hat and tie on his scarf. Fill with decorated sugar cookies and leave it near your stocking for Santa's snack.

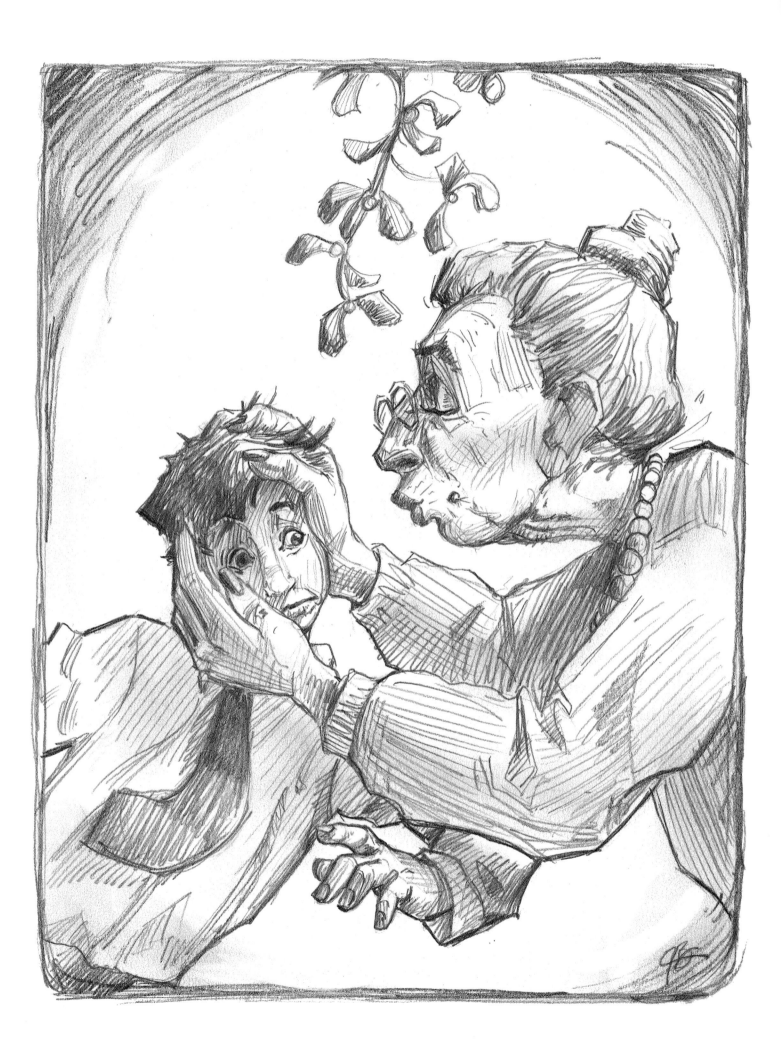

CHAPTER SEVEN

Christmas Eve

You've been counting the hours. Each day on your advent calendar is open except for one and it's finally here: Christmas Eve, the most magical night of the year. Every family has its own way of celebrating this wonderful evening. Some wait until that night to decorate the tree. Lights, ornaments, and tinsel are brought out of the closet and draped on the branches. But even those families that have their trees completely decorated are usually still seeing the finishing touches: "Put the angel ornament over there!" your brother shouts. "No!" you reply. "Over on that side." Just as the last bits of tinsel are draped over the branches, the doorbell rings.

Guests pour into the room: cousins, aunts, uncles, nephews, nieces, friends. Punch, eggnog, and Christmas cookies are served all around.

After the guests are gone, you make sure your stocking is in place over the fireplace. A fire is lit and the lights are dimmed, so that only the warm blaze and the bright glow of the Christmas-tree lights fill the room. The air smells of crisp pine. Everyone snuggles in front of the fire. After a few carols, Mom or Dad reaches for a book.

> ***'Twas the night before Christmas***
> ***When all through the house,***
> ***Not a creature was stirring,***
> ***Not even a mouse . . .***

Then it's off to bed. But who can sleep? After all, even as you crawl under the covers, you know that Santa and his sleigh are soaring through the sky. Sometime during the night he or one of his elves will slip down your chimney and leave you your gifts.

> Heap on more wood! the wind is chill;
> But, let it whistle as it will,
> We'll keep our merry Christmas Eve still.
>
>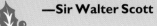
> —**Sir Walter Scott**

The Storke she rose on Christmas Eve

And sayed unto her broode,

I nowe muste fare to Bethlehem

To view the Sonne of God.

—**English Christmas Eve carol**

Burn, Yule log, burn!

Joy! Joy!

God gives us joy.

Noel comes! All blessings come!

May God let us see another year;

And if there are no more of us,

May our numbers be no less!

—**French carol**

Hear the sleighs with the bells—

Silver bells!

What world of merriment their
    melody foretells!

How they tinkle, tinkle, tinkle,

In the icy air of night!

While the stars, that oversprinkle

All the heavens, seem to twinkle

With crystalline delight

Keeping time, time, time

In a sort of Runic rhyme,

To the tintinnabulation that so
    musically wells

From the bells, bells, bells, bells,

Bells, bells, bells—

From the jingling and the tinkling of
    the bells.

—**Edgar Allan Poe**

But somehow . . . you doze off . . . toss and turn, then wake up right at the crack of dawn. Soon everyone is awake and the family gathers at the top of the stairs, and then you all race to the tree to see what surprises Santa has left.

There are as many different ways to celebrate Christmas Eve as there are families. And many cultures have their own special traditions. In France, a Yule log is burned each Christmas Eve, and the ashes are saved for good luck. In Sweden, an older brother or uncle enters the house dressed up as Jultomten, the Swedish version of Santa Claus (complete with red suit and white beard) and gives out gifts. In the Netherlands, there is a long-standing tradition of playing horns on Christmas Eve. All evening, the beautiful, round sound echoes across the land.

Any way it is celebrated, Christmas Eve is a special night. Nothing is more exciting than the rise of anticipation as all the pieces are put in place: the family gathers, the tree is trimmed, the fire lit, songs are sung, poems read. Finally, as you head to bed, you take one last look at the stockings, waiting to be filled with goodies, the tree, begging to be circled with presents.

Now, if you could only get to sleep. . . .

The Nutcracker, the magical story of a little girl's candy-filled Christmas Eve adventures, is a famous ballet written by Pyotr Ilich Tchaikovsky (pee-OH-ter ILL-itch cheye-KOF-skee) in 1892. Today, practically every city in the world hosts its own version each Christmas season. For many, a Christmas without the Nutcracker, the sugar-plum fairies, or the marzipan castle would almost be like Christmas without Santa!

The burning of the Yule log is an ancient Christmas tradition still practiced throughout most of Europe. A large log (usually oak) is cut and placed on the fire to burn for all twelve days of Christmas. This is believed to bring good luck for the coming year. After Christmas, the ash of the log is carefully saved and used to light the next year's log.

Walnut Brittle

Years ago, nuts were a traditional "stocking stuffer." Today, you can use nuts to make a special Christmas Eve treat.

**WHAT YOU'LL NEED
FOR FOUR POUNDS OF BRITTLE:**

A medium-sized saucepan, a candy thermometer, and two cookie pans, lightly coated with butter

INGREDIENTS:

1 cup white corn syrup

4 cups sugar

5 cups walnuts, other nuts, such as pecans or peanuts, or a mix

1 1/2 tablespoons unsalted butter

2 1/2 teaspoons baking soda

DIRECTIONS:

1. Place the syrup and sugar in a saucepan over medium heat. Stir constantly, until the sugar is melted.

2. Place the candy thermometer in the saucepan and continue cooking, without stirring, until the candy thermometer reads 240 degrees.

Be sure to let Mom or Dad help you with the candy thermometer—it can get very hot!

3. Add the nuts. Keep on cooking, stirring now and then, until the candy thermometer reads 300 degrees.

4. Remove the saucepan from the heat—remember to use potholders—and add the butter and baking soda right away. Stir well to blend. Don't be surprised if the mixture foams a little bit.

5. Pour half of the mixture into each of the pans and let it cool for at least 2 hours.

6. Use a knife to cut the candy into pieces. Make sure to let the candy sit another two hours before storing it in an airtight container.

The Nutcracker

BY E.T. HOFFMAN; RETOLD BY DAN ELISH

Christmas Eve was always a special night for Fritz and Marie. This year their tree was ten feet high, decorated from bottom to top with ornaments that glittered, shimmered, and sparkled. Underneath were piles of gifts in bright paper—red, green, and shining blue. Marie could hardly wait until morning to open those beautiful packages and see what was inside.

Rap! Rap! Rap!

Marie's heart jumped. Those knocks could only mean one thing. Her father, Mr. Stahlbaum, opened the door.

"Why, if it isn't Uncle Dosselmeier!" he exclaimed.

Marie jumped up. Yes, there he was! And what a strange man! Uncle Dosselmeier's back was hunched. A purple cape fell loosely around his shoulders. Over his left eye was a black patch.

"Greetings!" he cried, stepping into the house as he shook the snow off his shoulders. "A merry Christmas, isn't it? And a cold one, too! But that's all for the best! Of course it is! Eggnog? Yes, thank you! Don't mind if I do. Yes, a full cup, all the way to the top. And those sugar cookies!" He grabbed a handful. "There we are! Hmmm . . . Scrumptious!"

Uncle Dosselmeier soon found his way into an easy chair, then gestured to Fritz and Marie. The two children ran toward him. Each year their strange uncle brought them an odd but wonderful gift.

This year's lay across his open palm: a toy soldier, six inches long, complete with ornate blue uniform, boots, and sword.

"Wow!" Fritz said, grabbing the doll.

Uncle Dosselmeier smiled, exposing an uneven set of teeth. "It's a nutcracker!" he exclaimed. "Pass me a walnut, Marie! Now watch!"

And he opened the soldier's mouth, popped in the walnut, then snapped it shut, breaking the walnut shell—smack!—in two.

"Let me try!" Fritz begged, grabbing for the largest walnut in the tray.

"Not one so big, Fritz darling," cautioned his mother. "You don't want to break the . . ."

But Fritz crammed the walnut into the soldier's mouth.

"Watch it!" Marie cried.

Smash!

The walnut, too large for the little soldier's mouth, cracked the toy's jaw in two.

"Fool!" Marie hissed.

Fritz shrugged. "It's just a dumb soldier. . . ."

As the rest of the family gathered around the fire, Marie found a piece of pink rib-bon and tied it delicately around the soldier's jaw. Later, as her parents hustled her upstairs to bed, she left the toy standing majestically under the Christmas tree.

After midnight, when the house was still and the half moon bright, Marie woke with a start. She slipped on a robe, crept past her parents' room, and made her way down-stairs. She didn't know why, but she had to see her little nutcracker.

The living room was dark, but she could see the soldier, illuminated by a thin white moonbeam.

With her heart pounding, Marie inched toward the toy. The grandfather clock struck one in the morning. Outside, an old owl hooted.

"Hello, Marie," said a voice.

Marie jumped.

"Who said that?"

"I did!"

"Who?"

"Me!"

Marie's eyes went wide. What was this! The nutcracker's jaw was mended and the little man had a broad smile across his face. He took a stride forward and began marching in place.

"What are you doing?" Marie asked.

"Getting ready," the nutcracker replied.

"Ready for what?"

Before the soldier could answer, Marie heard a horrible rustling under the tree. She looked up. Scurrying across the floor was an entire army of mice!

"Ahh!" Marie cried, and leaped onto a chair. Then she noticed something worse. Lurching toward the nutcracker was the largest mouse of all, the Mouse King, a hideous seven-headed beast. He had a gold crown on each head and his fourteen red eyes blazed through the darkness.

"So we finally meet," the Mouse King hissed to the nutcracker, exposing seven sets of ragged, yellow teeth.

"Indeed!" the nutcracker said, drawing his sword.

The mice drew closer, surrounding the nutcracker.

"You're horribly outnumbered!" Marie cried to her little soldier.

"A minor problem!"

"They'll kill you!"

"I laugh at danger!" the brave soldier replied. "A mouse with seven heads? Ha!" The nutcracker wheeled around. "Troops! Charge!"

Suddenly, out of the walls stormed an entire army of toy soldiers, armed with sugar-plum-firing rifles.

Two soldiers set up a cannon.

Boom! A hazelnut shot through the air and plowed down a row of advancing mice.

Boom! And another row of mice fell.

The battle raged, but soon the mice were overwhelmed.

"Cowardly fools!" the seven-headed king cried. "Don't retreat!"

It was no use. The mice hustled back into the walls, though one brave one kicked the nutcracker's sword across the room as he scurried away. The Mouse King smiled, fourteen eyes shifting madly, hundreds of whiskers twitching. "It's just you and me now, little man!"

"Let's chew his legs off!" the sixth head suggested.

"No!" replied the second head, red eyes gleaming. "Let's stab him to death first!"

"Impossible!" the fourth head declared. "We must nibble at his arms, then gnaw at his boots!"

As the Mouse King argued with itself, Marie crept across the room, her heart pounding. She found the nutcracker's sword and quickly threw it across the room into his waiting hand.

Swish! Swish! Swish! Swish! Swish! Swish! Swish!

Seven strokes and the Mouse King was dead. Seven crowns lay on the ground before the Christmas tree. Marie looked up. The nutcracker, her nutcracker, was no wooden toy, but had been transformed, magically, into a handsome prince. When their eyes met, he bowed low to the ground.

"I've been under the curse of that miserable mouse for years," he said. "You saved me." His blue eyes sparkled. He took Marie's hand. "Come with me to my kingdom. It's time to celebrate!"

With a flash, the living room was gone! Marie gasped, for before her was a beautiful castle with four turrets raised proudly toward the gleaming sun. The air smelled of lemon peel and sweet cinnamon. The sky was deep blue. Candy canes grew from the ground.

"What a place!" Marie said, looking around her.

"My candy kingdom," the prince replied, stroking his thin mustache. "A land of sweets!" He shrugged. "It's not a bad life."

"I bet it's not."

"Now come to my Marzipan Castle!"

And the prince led Marie across a moat flowing with honey, decorated with giant chocolate crocodiles. Townspeople, dressed in peppermint suits, cookie-dough dresses, and icing hats lined the streets and cheered.

Inside the main hall of the castle a band played. Four young women whisked across the room.

"Oh, my brother!" they cried. "You're free!"

"Yes," the prince said, hugging them all. "It's all Marie's doing! She helped me break the magic curse!" He looked around the royal hall with the walls painted a beautiful turquoise, the floor a shimmering green. "This sure beats being the slave of a seven-headed mouse!"

Everyone laughed and they all introduced themselves to Marie. Then they invited her into the banquet hall, where waiters dressed in caramel tuxedos served a feast, as a band of candy-cane saxophones and vanilla-coated tubas played. After dessert, there was a game of castle-wide tag. There were many interesting and sweet places to hide: behind giant gumdrops, inside chocolate chests. Then, finally, it was time to sleep.

Four royal attendants led Marie to a private chamber where she collapsed onto a marshmallow-stuffed bed. In seconds, she was fast asleep.

"Marie, honey! Wake up!"

Marie stirred. It was her mother! She sat up with a start.

"Mother . . .?" Marie asked. "How did *you* get here?"

Mrs. Stahlbaum laughed. "How did I get here? I live here."

And Marie looked around her. She was in *her* room. All traces of the prince and castle were gone. She shook herself.

"Oh, Mother," she said, eyes wide. "What a night. First, I saved the nutcracker from the Mouse King and then . . . then I went to a kingdom made up of sweets!"

Mrs. Stahlbaum smiled. "What a nice dream to have on Christmas Eve," she said. "Now hurry up. Your brother is already opening his presents!"

Maybe it was just a dream, Marie thought disappointedly, as her mother left the room.

Downstairs she could hear the sound of her brother ripping wrapping paper. Downhearted, she slipped out of bed, but then something glittering on her night table caught her eye. Marie's heart jumped! Seven tiny, golden crowns from the Mouse King!

Trembling, she picked them up and a tear of pure joy rolled down her cheek.

It *was* true! she thought. What a Christmas! What a wonderful Christmas!

Picture Frames You Can Share

When Christmas comes, families get together—aunts, uncles, cousins, grandparents, and old friends. What better gift for people you haven't seen in a long time than your picture in a frame you made yourself. Use a school photo, a snapshot taken during last summer's vacation, or a family photo taken this Christmas.

MATERIALS:

Two sheets of cardboard, cut to size, if necessary: 8-1/2 x 11 inches for a 5 x 7 inch print, 9 x 7 inches for a 3 x 5 inch print, 4 x 4 inches for a wallet-size print

Ruler

Pencil

A photo of you

Scissors with a sharp point (ask an adult to help you with these)

2 sheets of wrapping paper

Glue stick

Colored poster board

1. Ask an adult to help you cut the cardboard to the size for your picture, then cut ¼ inch off the edges of one piece to make it smaller than the other. This is the back piece now.

2. Use a ruler to connect the opposite corners of the bigger piece of cardboard and draw a line. Draw another line crossing this one connecting the other two corners. The center of the X is the center of the cardboard. Do this on the back of your photo, also.

3. Place the X on your photo on the X on the cardboard, then trace the photo. Using the ruler, draw another line ¼ inch inside the picture outline.

4. Cut along the inside line with the scissors. If you need help with this, ask an adult. Start by poking a hole in the center and cutting straight into the corners. Then cut the straight sides of the opening. This is the front of your frame.

5. Lay the front of your frame on the wrong side of the wrapping paper, and trace around the outside edge. Measure and draw a line 1 inch on the outside of this one. Then cut the wrapping paper along the outside line.

6. Put the cardboard frame on the inside line on the paper, and put glue around the edge of the back side of the frame. Fold the corners of the wrapping paper over the corners of the frame, then fold the sides down.

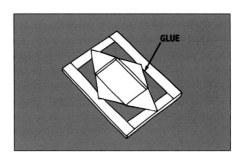

7. With your scissors, poke a hole in the paper at the center of the frame's opening and then cut straight to the corners. The cuts will look like an X, and the pieces of paper like four triangles. Put some glue around the edge of the opening and fold the triangular pieces to the back of the frame.

8. Lay the other piece of cardboard on the wrong side of the wrapping paper. Trace around the cardboard, then measure and draw a line 1 inch from the traced line. Cut along the outside line. Spread glue around the edges of the cardboard and fold the corners then paper edges down to glue them flat.

9. Lay the back on the wrapping paper again and trace it. Then measure and draw a line ½ inch inside the traced line. Cut along the inside line. Glue this piece over the back, making sure to cover up the glued-down edges.

10. Now you are ready to glue the front to the back of the frame. Put glue around three sides of the back piece and glue it to the back of the front piece. This will leave one side open. Slide the photo into the frame.

11. To make an easel so the frame will stand up, cut a piece of poster board ½ inch smaller than your frame. Find the center of one long side by measuring it. Make a line from this center mark to each opposite corner. Fold along these lines to form a center triangle with two triangular flaps on each side.

12. To attach the easel to the back of the frame, line up the bottom edge of the easel with the bottom of the frame. Line up the point of the center triangle with the center of the frame and glue it to the back of your frame.

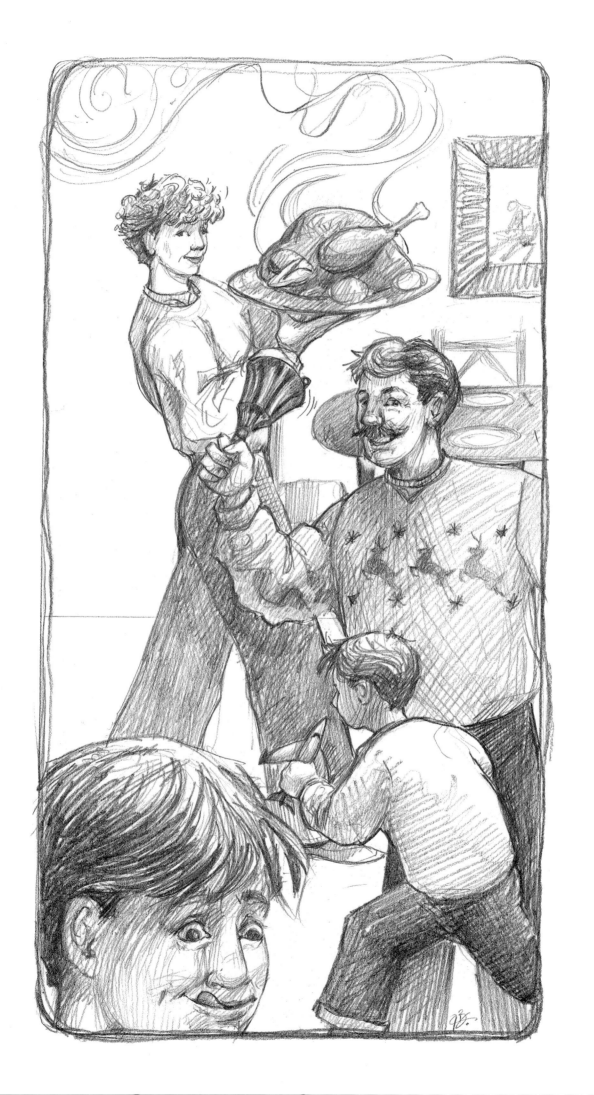

CHAPTER EIGHT

Christmas Dinner

Wrapping paper is in piles on the floor around the Christmas tree and your gifts have all been opened. You've tried out (or on) as many of your presents as you could, and you've admired your brother's and your sister's stash. You've said many thank-yous and have gotten many in return.

But the thrill of the day isn't over yet. In many ways the best is yet to come: Christmas dinner.

"Quick," your mother or father says. "Let's clean up this mess!"

The whole family springs into action, throwing out or saving wrapping paper, piling presents under the tree. Then, the doorbell rings and cousins, uncles, aunts, and friends arrive.

By now, you can smell the tasty aroma of turkey or goose coming from the oven. As some of the adults bustle around the room, setting the table, you exchange a few more gifts with a cousin or two. Then you are summoned to the kitchen to help bring serving bowls and plates into the dining room. And finally, your father announces, "Dinner's on!"

This is the meal of the year! Turkey, stuffing, cranberry sauce, mashed potatoes, peas, gravy—and much, much more.

After grace is said, with a special word for those who aren't lucky enough to enjoy such a marvelous feast, you dig in. The excitement of Christmas Eve, plus a morning of presents, makes one very hungry. Then it's time for dessert—apple and pumpkin pie, fruit cakes, and more Christmas cookies.

The Boar's Head Carol

The boar's head in hand bear I,
Bedecked with bays and rosemary;
And I pray you, my masters, be merry,
You who are at this feast.

The boar's head, as I understand,
Is the rarest dish in all this land,
Which thus bedecked with gay garland
Let us serve by singing.

Our steward hath provided this,
In honor of the King of Bliss,
Which on this day to be served is,
In the royal hall.

—Traditional English carol

We Gather Together

We gather together to ask the Lord's blessing.

He chastens and hastens His will to make known.

The wicked oppressing now cease to be distressing.

Sing praises to His name for He forgets not His own.

—a traditional hymn
(to give thanks for food)

Yule! Yule!

Yule! Yule!

Three puddings in a pool;

Crack nuts and cry Yule!

—Anonymous

Ceremonies for Christmas

Cut now the white loaf here,

The while the meat is shredding;

For the rare mince pie

And plums stand by

To fill the paste that's a-kneading.

—Robert Herrick

As much fun as it is to eat the meal, it can be just as enjoyable to be involved in making it. It's great to help Mom or Dad baste the turkey, whip the sweet potatoes, or stir the batter for Christmas cookies.

As with every other part of Christmas, Christmas dinner contains its own share of traditions. In Sweden, the whole family gathers in the kitchen before the great meal. Everybody spears a piece of dark bread on a fork, dips it into a kettle of broth, and eats it along with a piece of meat. This is done to wish for "luck" in the coming year. In eastern Europe, a place at the table is left free in case Jesus Christ might want to join the party. In Norway, some say the heat of the ovens baking the Christmas cookies melts the heavy snows outside!

When the meal is through, Christmas is close to officially over. The excitement of Christmas Eve, the thrill of Christmas morning, and the satisfaction of a great dinner, has made for a wonderful holiday.

After a warm good-bye to friends, there are many dishes to clear and wash, but it is certainly all worth the effort. This is a special meal that comes around only once a year.

As you crawl into bed that night, you know that starting tomorrow, it'll be back to regular dinners. But you'll still remember this wonderful Christmas for the rest of the year. Time passes by quickly enough and soon it'll be time to eat turkey again!

The English have a Christmas tradition that revolves around making plum pudding. Every member of the family must stir the pudding and make a secret wish. This is thought to bring good luck for the coming year.

Every family has their own recipe for plum pudding. But as an old Englishwoman once put it, "Put plenty of good things in, my dear, and plenty of good things will come out!"

I know you've heard of cattle drives, but have you ever heard of turkey drives? Well, in 1863, before the age of refrigeration, a man and two boys drove a flock of five hundred turkeys six hundred miles from Missouri to Denver! They got the birds into the young city just in time for the Christmas feast.

Cranberry Sauce

There are some foods without which the Christmas table just wouldn't seem right. Of course, there are the obvious things—the turkey or goose, the stuffing, the pies—but often it's the little things that make Christmas dinner complete.

One of those things is cranberry sauce. Bright red, it adds color to the feast and a sweet-tart taste to the meal. This recipe serves 8.

WHAT YOU'LL NEED:

A medium-sized saucepan

INGREDIENTS:

2 cups sugar

2 cups water

4 cups (1 lb.) cranberries

DIRECTIONS:

1. Mix the sugar into the water.

2. Bring the mixture to a boil, stirring occasionally.

3. When the sugar has dissolved completely, add the cranberries. After 3 or 4 minutes, they should begin to pop.

4. Remove the mixture from the heat and stir.

It's that simple. Let your cranberry sauce cool, then refrigerate it until it's time for Christmas dinner. If you're feeling adventurous, perhaps you can make a mold and shape your cranberry sauce into reindeer or Christmas trees.

A Christmas Carol

BY CHARLES DICKENS ; ABRIDGED

Such a bustle ensued that you might have thought a turkey the rarest of all birds, a feathered phenomenon, to which a black swan was a matter of course—and in truth it was something very like it in that house. Mrs. Cratchit made the gravy (ready beforehand in a little saucepan) hissing hot, Master Peter mashed the potatoes with incredible vigor, Miss Belinda sweetened up the applesauce, Martha dusted the hot plates, Bob took Tiny Tim beside him in a tiny corner at the table, the two young Cratchits set chairs for everybody, not forgetting themselves, and mounting guard upon their posts, crammed spoons into their mouths, lest they should shriek for goose before their turn came to be helped. At last the dishes were set on, and grace was said. It was succeeded by a breathless pause, as Mrs. Cratchit, looking slowly all along the carving knife, prepared to plunge it in the breast, but when she did, and when the long-expected gush of stuffing issued forth, one murmur of delight arose all round the board; and even Tiny Tim, excited by the two young Cratchits, beat on the table with the handle of his knife, and feebly cried: "Hurrah!"

There never was such a goose. Bob said he didn't believe there ever was such a goose cooked. Its tenderness and flavor were the themes of universal admiration. Eked out by applesauce and mashed potatoes, it was a sufficient dinner for the whole family; indeed, as Mrs. Cratchit said with great delight (surveying one small atom of a bone upon the dish), they hadn't ate it all at last! Yet everyone had enough, and the youngest Cratchits in particular were steeped in sage and onion to the eyebrows! But now, the plates being changed by Miss Belinda, Mrs. Cratchit left the room alone—too nervous to bear witness—to take the pudding up, and bring it in.

Suppose it should not be done enough! Suppose it should break in turning out! Suppose somebody should have got over the wall of the backyard and stolen it while they were merry with the goose—a supposition at which the two young Cratchits became livid! All sorts of horrors were supposed.

Hallo! A great deal of steam! The pudding was out of the copper. A smell like a washing day! That was the cloth. A smell like an eating house and a pastry cook's next

door to each other, with a laundress's next door to that! That was the pudding! In half a minute Mrs. Cratchit entered—flushed, but smiling proudly—with the pudding, like a speckled cannonball, so hard and firm, blazing in half of half a quartern of ignited brandy, and bedlight with Christmas holly stuck into the top.

Oh, a wonderful pudding! Bob Cratchit said, and calmly, too, that he regarded it as the greatest success achieved by Mrs. Cratchit since their marriage. Mrs. Cratchit said that, now the weight was off her mind, she would confess she had her doubts about the quantity of flour. Everybody had something to say about it, but nobody said or thought it was at all a small pudding for a large family. It would have been flat heresy to do. Any Cratchit would have blushed to hint at such a thing.

At last the dinner was all done, the cloth was cleared, the hearth swept, and the fire made up. The compound in the jug being tasted, and considered perfect, apples and oranges were put upon the table, and a shovelful of chestnuts on the fire. Then all the Cratchit family drew round the hearth in what Bob Cratchit called a circle, meaning half a one, and at Bob Cratchit's elbow stood the family display of glass: two tumblers and a custard cup without a handle.

These held the hot stuff from the jug, however, as well as golden goblets would have done, and Bob served it out with beaming looks, while the chestnuts on the fire sputtered and crackled noisily. Then Bob proposed:

"A merry Christmas to us all, my dears. God bless us!"

Which all the family reechoed.

"God bless us, every one!" said Tiny Tim, the last of all.

Christmas Dinner Placemats

Adorn your Christmas dinner table with place mats you make yourself. Decorate them with the names of family and friends and use them as place cards, too.

MATERIALS:

Construction, wrapping, or origami paper

Scissors

Glue stick

Hold punch

Foil stars

1 yard of self-stick plastic per place mat

Ruler

1. Lay out one large sheet or several small sheets of paper to measure about 13 x 18 inches, the size of a place mat. Use just a little glue from the glue stick along the over-laping edges to hold the sheets together.

2. Make up any design for your place mat. You can draw houses, animals, people, trees, or even dinosaurs, and cut them out of different-colored paper. Using a paper hole punch you can make dot-shaped snow. Lots of different-colored dots will look like confetti. Foil stars add shine.

3. Glue down the large pieces of your design. Leave the dots from the hole punch where they fall. They will be held down by the plastic covering.

4. Cut a piece of self-stick plastic a little bit larger than the place mat and peel off the backing. Tape it to your work-table with the sticky side up. Lay the place mat on the plastic and press it down.

5. Cut another sheet of plastic, the same size as the first. Peel off about 2 inches of backing along one edge. Lay this edge on the mat and smooth out the bubbles from the center to the edges. Keep unpeeling the backing as the plastic covers the mat.

6. To make the sides of your mat straight, lay a ruler along the edges of your mat outside your design and draw lines on the plastic. Cut along the lines with scissors.

Index